YOU MUST ENDURE

You Must Endure

The Lancashire Loyals in Japanese captivity, 1942–1945

Chris Given-Wilson

First published in 2021
by Palatine Books,
Carnegie House,
Chatsworth Road
Lancaster LA1 4SL
www.palatinebooks.com

Copyright © Chris Given-Wilson

All rights reserved
Unauthorised duplication contravenes existing laws

The right of Chris Given-Wilson to be identified as the author of this work has been asserted in accordance with the Copyright, Designs and Patents act 1988

British Library Cataloguing-in-Publication data
A catalogue record for this book is available from the British Library

Paperback ISBN 13: 978-1-910837-35-1

Designed and typeset by Carnegie Book Production
www.carnegiebookproduction.com

Printed and bound by Severn

Front cover illustrations: 'Col. Noguchi welcoming the POWs to Keijo Camp', in Toze and Strange, *In Defence of Singapore* (Preston, 1947); Lancashire Loyals' cap badge, Mike Young, northeastmedals.co.uk.
Back cover illustrations: Pencil portrait of 2nd Lt Patrick 'Paddy' Given-Wilson, by Captain Donald Teale, Keijo Camp, May 1944; 'Albert at Changi', from *NIB*, Christmas 1942.

Table of Contents

Preface	vii
Principal sources	xi
Abbreviations and illustrations	xii
Chapter 1: Lion City	1
Prisoner stories: 'James'	15
Chapter 2: *Fukai Maru*	17
Prisoner stories: Gunner Starkey	31
Chapter 3: Endurance	35
Prisoner stories: Bombardier Butler	55
Chapter 4: Insincerity	59
Prisoner stories: Dr Mizuguchi	71
Chapter 5: Rank	75
Prisoner stories: Artists	91
Chapter 6: *Mainichi*	97
Prisoner stories: 'Their Nibs'	113
Chapter 7: 'Not necessarily to Japan's advantage'	119
Prisoner stories: 'My first uncensored letter for three and a half years!'	126
Retrospect: 'The hinge of fate'	129
Bibliography	138
Endnotes	140

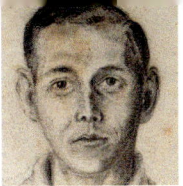

Preface

AT LEAST NINETY PER CENT of British books, films or television documentaries on the Second World War are about the war in Europe, ten per cent or less on the war in the Pacific. Given that Winston Churchill described the fall of Singapore in February 1942 as 'the worst disaster and largest capitulation in British history', and that Japan posed a greater direct threat than Germany or Italy to what most Britons of the time regarded as the nation's crowning achievement – the British Empire – such an imbalance is at first sight surprising. However, the reasons are not hard to find: firstly, because although it was Japan that imperilled the Empire, it was Germany that imperilled Britain; secondly, because most of the British troops who fought the Japanese suffered a humiliating defeat and were never given the chance to redeem themselves – a bit like Dunkirk without D-Day. Apart from the 'Forgotten Army' in Burma, it was very largely the United States that defeated Japan, at a cost of over 100,000 American lives. For the British, the memories were painful, the truths uncomfortable. As a result, there has been one of those witting or unwitting acts of not remembering which can shape a nation's understanding of its history as much as the time-honoured rituals of commemoration.

There are, of course, a few infamous events of the Pacific War that are not forgotten, such as the building of the Death Railway between Thailand and Burma in 1942–3 which, by virtue of a succession of films, histories and novels (*The Bridge on the River Kwai*, *The Railway Man*, *The Narrow Road to the Deep North*), remains for many people one of the defining images of World War II captivity. By comparison, the stories of other Allied prisoners of the Japanese remain relatively unknown, even when well-documented. This is certainly true of the camp at Seoul (renamed Keijo by the Japanese after they annexed Korea), which is barely mentioned even in comprehensive histories of Japanese POW camps. I too would undoubtedly have remained ignorant of it had not my father, a junior officer with the 2nd battalion of the Loyal North Lancashire Regiment, spent three years as a prisoner there.

Pencil portrait of my father, 2nd Lt Patrick 'Paddy' Given-Wilson, by Captain Donald Teale, Keijo Camp, May 1944

Hoping to provide some relief for their fellow prisoners, my father and two other British POWs at Keijo edited and illustrated a magazine which they called *Nor Iron Bars* (from the seventeenth-century poet Richard Lovelace's *To Althea, from Prison*: 'Stone walls do not a prison make/Nor iron bars a cage'). Japanese camp officials were suspicious of anything written by their prisoners, and had they discovered *Nor Iron Bars*, which was consistently subversive and often openly hostile in tone, there would have been a price to pay. Fortunately, the POWs managed to conceal it and, when Japan surrendered, brought it back with them to the Lancashire Infantry Museum, Fulwood Barracks, Preston. Here it has remained ever since, largely ignored, although some illustrations from it were included in a short book on art produced by Lancashire POWs, recognition of the fact that there were several artists of real talent at Seoul.[1] Indeed, *Nor Iron Bars* is as notable for the quality of some of its artwork as for its written content.

Apart from *Nor Iron Bars*, the Lancashire Infantry Museum houses many other original documents relating to the 2nd Loyals' experiences during and after the fall of Singapore and their captivity at Keijo, and I am grateful to the staff of the Museum for giving me unrestricted access to their archives and in particular for allowing me to make a photographic copy of *Nor Iron Bars* from which to work. I am also grateful to those who read earlier drafts of this book and offered useful suggestions, and to my brother Patrick and sister Rosalind for contributing in various ways to its publication.

Although my father, an editor of considerable modesty, is largely anonymous in the sources I have used to write this book, it is dedicated to his memory, along with those Allied soldiers who shared his captivity, and their families.

Principal sources

This book is largely based on original sources dating from the years 1941 to 1947. The most important are:

(1) *Nor Iron Bars* (*NIB*): a magazine produced by three officers of the 2nd Battalion, the Loyal Regiment (my father, Capt. John Turner and Lt Tom Henling Wade), during their captivity at Changi and Keijo, 1942–5, now in Lancashire Infantry Museum. Fourteen issues were produced, totalling 516 pages. The pages are not numbered, but footnote references are given to the issues, which were first produced at Changi on 6 and 16 April 1942, in May 1942, June 1942 and July 1942, and then at Keijo as follows: Christmas 1942, January 1943, February 1943, April 1943, July 1943, Christmas 1943, Easter 1944, Christmas 1944 and April 1945.

(2) John Lever's Diary (JLD): Diary written by Capt. John Lever of the Loyal Regiment during his captivity at Keijo, September 1942 to September 1945, now in the Lancashire Infantry Museum. The 119 handwritten pages are not numbered, but entries are in chronological order under monthly headings, to which references are given in the footnotes.

(3) International Military Tribunal for the Far East (IMT): the official transcript of the war crimes trial of 'Noguchi et al.' at United States Eighth Army Headquarters, Yokohama, 4 June to 15 September 1947 (81 pp.): www.online.uni-marburg.de/icwc/yokohama/Yokohama%20No.%20T181.pdf

The account of his captivity by Tom Henling Wade, who spent just over a year in Keijo Camp (1942–3) until transferred to Japan, is also a useful source, although it was not published until 1994.

Abbreviations

AIF	Australian Imperial Force
CED	Colonel Elrington's Diary (LIM)
CHJ	*The Cambridge History of Japan, Volume 6: The Twentieth Century*, ed. Peter Duus (Cambridge, 1988)
DJE	*The Dismantling of Japan's Empire in the East*, ed. B. Kushner and S. Muminov (New York, 2017)
DFS	Brian Farrell, *The Defence and Fall of Singapore* (Singapore, 2005)
IDS	A. V. Toze and S. Strange, *In Defence of Singapore* (Preston, 1947)
IMT	International Military Tribunal for the Far East
IWM	Imperial War Museum, London
JLD	John Lever's Diary (LIM)
LIM	Lancashire Infantry Museum, Fulwood Barracks, Preston
NIB	*Nor Iron Bars* (LIM)
POJ	Tom Henling Wade, *Prisoner of the Japanese: from Changi to Tokyo* (Kangaroo Press, Kenthurst, Australia)
SPK	J. D. Wilkinson, *Sketches of a POW in Korea* (Melbourne, 1945)
STS	Brian MacArthur, *Surviving the Sword: Prisoners of the Japanese 1942–45* (London, 2005)
WAJ	S. Woodburn Kirby, *The War Against Japan, Volume 5: The Surrender of Japan* (London, 1969)

Illustrations

All the figures in this book are contemporary, taken mainly from *Nor Iron Bars*, which was extensively illustrated with sketches and cartoons. Many of them were done by Capt. Donald Teale of the Loyal Regiment, an accomplished portraitist and cartoonist. Pte

Harry Kingsley of the Loyals also left many excellent sketches of his time at Keijo, some of which are now in the Imperial War Museum, London. Two sketchbooks in story-board format, both published within two years of the end of the war, have also provided a number of illustrations: *Sketches of a POW in Korea* (*SPK*), by Corporal John Wilkinson of the AIF, and *In Defence of Singapore* (*IDS*), by Sergeant S. Strange of the Loyals and Bombardier A. V. Toze of 122 Field Regiment, Royal Artillery.

Given the challenging conditions in which the illustrations were produced and the quality of the materials available (wrapping paper from Red Cross parcels, unused naval messaging pads, etc.), they have stood the test of time remarkably well, a tribute to the care taken to preserve them at the Infantry Museum. Inevitably, however, some have yellowed and a few are stained. A few photographs were also inserted in *Nor Iron Bars*, taken by the Kempeitai (Japanese military police) for propaganda purposes. These are grainy and sometimes blurred, taken with cameras which themselves might now be museum exhibits, but they are authentic.

Capt. John Lever at Keijo Camp, by Harry Kingsley

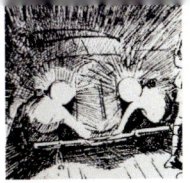

ONE

Lion City

On the morning of 7 September 1945, a jeep carrying three American officers drove up to the gates of the stockaded compound in Keijo (Seoul) which for the past three years had served as Number One Prisoner of War Camp in Japanese-occupied Korea. Three weeks had passed since Japan's surrender, yet apart from a leaflet dropped from an American B-29 advising POWs what to do in the event of a Japanese capitulation, they had received no word about liberation. Listless and frustrated, the 166 prisoners at Keijo – 142 British, eleven Russian, eleven Australian and two American – feared a 'bust-up' unless something happened soon. And for one British officer, Lt Roger Pigott, the delay proved fatal: debilitated by tubercular meningitis following two years in Keijo civilian jail, he died on 29 August. It was thus with relief as much as elation that Col. Mordaunt 'Bill' Elrington, the senior British officer at Keijo, walked out to greet the liberators at the gate. But the American commander was in no mood for formalities: 'Say, colonel,' he began, 'who d'ya want shot?'[1]

This was not an idle question. In Borneo, Australian troops so sickened at the condition of Allied prisoners brought from Java killed any Japanese they found. At Bougainville on the Solomon Islands, Japanese soldiers who had mustered to surrender were simply machine-gunned.[2] In fact, none of the guards at Keijo was executed, although several of them were later tried for war crimes by the International Military Tribunal for the Far East, and given prison terms of up to thirty-seven years with hard labour.[3] Yet the fact that many of the 920 Japanese war criminals who *were* subsequently hanged had worked as prison-camp officials is not surprising, given that the death rate among Japan's Allied prisoners – almost all fit young men at the time of their capture – was a grim twenty-seven per cent (compared to four per cent in German prisoner-of-war camps).[4] Many of the survivors also died relatively young, their health undermined by malnutrition, medical negligence and casual brutality not infrequently culminating in torture. The reluctance of FEPOWs (Far East Prisoners of War) to talk about their experiences in captivity is well known, not only because their memories were too distressing, or because survivors were ordered on their return not to talk about their experiences of Japanese captivity, since the details might be too traumatic for relatives of those who had not survived,[5] but also because it was not easy for them to be seen to have had a 'good war' in the Far East. On the other hand, they were not unwilling to write about it. Diaries, memoirs and letters describing their experiences are numerous, many of them unpublished. Most of them begin, almost inescapably, with the Allied catastrophe with which their ordeal began, the fall of Singapore.

There is a certain symmetry to the fact that the Loyals at Keijo were among the last to be liberated following Japan's surrender, for three and a half years earlier in Singapore city they had also been the last to lay down their arms. The time was 7.40 p.m., the date 15 February 1942. The light was fading fast, the Allied forces were encircled, and the bombardment was relentless. Charged with defending the western approach road to the city at Pasir Panjang, soldiers of the Loyals' A Company spotted a group of Japanese on the ridge overlooking their HQ at Gillman barracks. A machine-gun was commandeered and a volley unleashed at the enemy, who quickly dispersed. These were almost certainly the last shots to be fired in the Allied defence of Singapore.[6] An hour later, a car puttered up from the barracks, headlights blazing. Greeted with cries of 'Put your bloody lights out!' the driver, Capt. Webber,[7] told them that was no longer necessary, since at 6.15 p.m. a cease-fire had been agreed, to come into effect at 8.30. The General Officer Commanding the British Commonwealth forces in Malaya, Lt-General Arthur Percival, had met his opposite number, Lt-General Tomoyuki Yamashita, at the Ford Motor Factory on Bukit Timah road and agreed to surrender unconditionally the

'Put your bloody lights out!' The moment of surrender (*IDS*)

following morning. Discarding their weapons, the Loyals quietly withdrew to their quarters, where they 'composed themselves as best they could for the silent ordeal of the night, numbed and galled by the bitterness of enforced surrender'.[8]

Ten weeks earlier, Britain and Japan had still nominally been at peace. It was between 1.00 and 2.00 a.m. on Monday 8 December 1941 when Japanese forces who had embarked in Indochina began landing in southern Thailand and northern Malaya – thus coinciding precisely with the blitzing of Pearl Harbour and the simultaneous attacks on Hong Kong, Guam and the Philippines.[9] Beachheads were rapidly established, accompanied by an aerial bombardment of the fighter bases in northern Malaya of such intensity that within twenty-four hours more than half of the 110 Allied planes stationed there were either destroyed or disabled.[10] Singapore island was also bombed on the morning of 8 December. That evening, hoping to intercept auxiliary Japanese forces, the battleship *Prince of Wales* and battlecruiser *Repulse*, accompanied by four destroyers, left Singapore's Keppel harbour and steamed northwards through the South China Sea. Doomed by lack of air support, both ships were sunk by Japanese torpedo-bombers some sixty miles off the east coast of Malaya shortly after midday on 10 December, with the loss of some 800 lives.[11] They were the first capital ships of any nation to be sunk solely by air power in the open sea: not a single Allied capital ship now remained operative between Hawaii and India. Three days after launching his 'driving charge' to destroy Western hegemony in south-east Asia, Yamashita had already gained almost undisputed ascendancy both in the air and at sea.

The defence of Malaya and Singapore thus became predominantly an infantry war – which meant, given the country's topography, jungle warfare. Some 450 miles from north to south and extending to a maximum width of 200 miles from east to west, Malaya was mostly tropical rainforest, rubber plantations and tin mines, 'close country' with severely restricted lines of fire but abundant opportunities for infiltration and outflanking manoeuvres. On the west coast, all the way from Singapore up to Bangkok, ran a railway line and trunk road connected by arteries to the main ports and towns, but the eastern half of the peninsula was dense, teeming jungle, with few serviceable access routes. The undulating landscape, marshy rivers and steamy equatorial climate also meant that moving heavy equipment was often a struggle. On the other hand, Malaya's estates and plantations were criss-crossed with rough tracks and footpaths, ideal terrain for the thousands of bicycles used by Japanese infantry, while coastal regions were honeycombed with creeks and inlets, frequently dissolving into mangrove swamp, which they also proved adept at exploiting.

On paper, the forces contesting the Malayan peninsula were quite evenly matched: Yamashita probably had a total of some 125,000 men at his disposal, Percival about 130,000 – although the numbers deployed at any given time were a fraction of this.[12] However, many of the Allied soldiers had only had a few days to acclimatize to the tropical conditions and were largely untrained in jungle warfare. It was, at any rate, not numerical superiority on the ground that accounted for the outcome of the campaign but the ferocity and tempo of the Japanese advance, aided by air and sea dominance. Night and day, they drove relentlessly forward, constantly surprising the Allies before they had time to regroup, prepare defensive lines, or bring up reinforcements. If Japanese

The Malayan Campaign 1941–2

forward patrols were ambushed, rather than withdrawing they would melt into the jungle before circling round to cut off the enemy's line of retreat, thereby isolating units and picking them off piecemeal. Like the Nazis' *blitzkrieg*, Japanese tactics focused on bringing overwhelming pressure to bear on selected points in the enemy's defence and refusing to retreat even when checked: thrust and envelopment, thrust and envelopment. Physical fitness also contributed to their greater mobility. As one of the Loyals put it, 'They not only carried their own equipment and food but also mortars and parts of 25-pounder guns strapped on their backs, thus enabling them to travel with far less transport than we required and to have a far greater proportion of actual fighting forces. Actually, we immobilised ourselves by having too much mobility.'[13] Such audacity naturally involved risk-taking: Japanese lines of supply and communication were overextended, patrols were sometimes annihilated, and casualties were high. Yet this was a price which both General Yamashita and his men seemed willing to pay. Allied commanders commented ruefully on the 'fanatical fury' and extraordinary bravery shown by Japanese soldiers: 'they always obeyed instructions to the letter and seemed to welcome death for their country'.

The pace of the Japanese advance was bewildering. By 18 December, within ten days of landing, they had already gained 150 miles, storming through the defensive lines of III Indian Corps at Jitra and Gurun and forcing the evacuation of Penang island, thus effectively driving the Allies out of northern Malaya. Three weeks on, a few days into the new year, they were more than half way down the peninsula. The effect on Allied morale was numbing: constantly on the run, exhausted but unable to sleep, hauling supplies and artillery up to the front only to haul them back a few days later (or simply destroy them in denial operations), digging trenches and erecting earthworks only to see them overrun, sometimes within hours, the men were pushing at the limit of their endurance. 'Officers and men moved like automata, and often could not grasp the simplest order.'[14] At Slim river, fifty miles north of Kuala Lumpur, where the convergence of railway, river and trunk road created a formidable defensive position, Percival decided to make a stand. It lasted just six hours:

at 3.30 a.m. on 7 January, in brilliant moonlight, thirty Japanese tanks and infantry transports approached directly down the road. When the leading tank hit a mine, the soldiers behind fanned out on loop roads and surrounded the defenders. By 9.30, the Japanese armoured column had advanced twenty-five miles, seizing the Slim river bridge (there having been insufficient time to blow it up), destroying one brigade and scattering another. The 'battle of Slim river' cost the Allies 450 killed and 3,000 captured.[15] Four days later, General Yamashita entered Kuala Lumpur unopposed, capturing a rich haul of what he liked to call 'Churchill supplies'. With Kuantan airfield on the east coast having been overrun a few days earlier, the Japanese now had bases on each side of central Malaya from which they could launch almost continuous bombing raids on Singapore, which they proceeded to do.[16]

Unrelenting humiliation on such a scale soon took its toll. Politicians and generals disagreed on strategy. The *sine qua non* was the preservation of the great naval base on the north coast of Singapore island, the linchpin of British imperial defence in the Far East – but how best to ensure this? Some Allied generals advocated withdrawal to Johore, where a narrower front could be defended in depth, but Percival wanted to contest 'every bend in the road' until sufficient reinforcements arrived to launch a counter-offensive. His relationship with Major-General Gordon Bennett, the prickly and controversial Australian commander, was especially difficult.[17] Following the Slim river fiasco, however, there was really no option left but to withdraw to Johore. The long-awaited reinforcements had at last begun to arrive on Singapore, allowing more troops to be sent up to the mainland, where Percival proposed to fight the 'main battle' along a line stretching from Muar in the west, via Segamat, to Mersing on the east coast. Among those who were now ordered up to this line were the 2nd Loyals, who for the past two years had been deployed on garrison duty in Singapore. They arrived at Segamat around 8.00 a.m. on Tuesday 13 January, spent two days 'digging, wiring and felling trees' to strengthen the town's defences, and were then moved up to the front. Barely had they arrived when the battle began. Malacca fell on the 14th, and two days later the Japanese crossed the river at Muar and seized the town. Yet again the Allies found themselves being mauled on every front, blowing bridges and fighting rear-guard actions as best they could. The action in northern Johore was close and vicious. By 25 January, the Loyals had suffered losses – killed, wounded, or missing – of almost one third of the battalion's strength (from around 750 down to 512)[18] and had been forced back to a position picketing the road west of Ayer Hitam. What happened there, as described by Col. Elrington, was almost a microcosm of the whole Allied debacle in Malaya:[19]

> By 16.00 hours a regular bombardment was going on, our mortars receiving special attention. This effort fizzled out by 18.00 hours; after the continuous noise of the afternoon, the complete silence that followed seemed unreal, yet it persisted long enough to impress on us the fact that the enemy had been definitely repulsed and to engender the thought that probably it was getting too late for a renewal of the attack. Suddenly, rudely and, as it seemed, profanely the quietude was shattered and the night made hideous by the clatter of machine guns from front, flank and rear. The banging of bombs, the crashing of shells through the trees, a crescendo of crackers and tommy-guns, the sharp spit of our Brens and the zip-crack of rifles pierced our ears as if all Bedlam were let loose. The Japanese must have, during the day, made a wide movement through the jungle away to our left flank and, at dusk, timed a complete surprise to the left and rear of our A Company, which was echeloned back across the road. The little Japs had percolated through the *ulu* [jungle] out of sight and sound and lay hidden by tall rushes where the marsh began. Some of them had ingeniously brought soap boxes to stand on when the moment came to open fire. Their machine guns were blazing away in extravagantly long bursts of fire sweeping all over the place, and the fusillade was continuous. There was no alternative to withdraw, and orders were issued accordingly. This was the position where we understood 'the big stand' of the war would be made to save Singapore. Ye gods!

At least the Loyals had not been at Parit Sulong, a few miles up the road, where the struggle for control of the bridge over the river Simpang developed into what one Japanese colonel later described as a 'war of extermination' between Japan's Imperial Guards and

4,500 Australian and Indian infantrymen, just 900 of whom returned. The Allies gave as good as they got at Parit Sulong, and the Japanese, stung by their losses, exacted retribution: 150 Australian and Indian soldiers too badly wounded to escape were rounded up and executed – some machine-gunned, some burned alive, some beaten to death.[20] Scenes such as this were becoming more common as the Japanese struggled to cope with their thousands of captives. Lance Corporal Busby was one of several Loyals trapped in a roadside swamp by eight Japanese tanks just north of Ayer Hitam:

> They hauled us out after one of my men was bayoneted in the scuffle. We were stripped of our arms and equipment and our pockets were rifled. They took not only our pay books and papers but also such things as pens, watches and other personal things. We were then motioned to sit down by the side of the road while some of the officers had a very short conference as to our fate. After about two minutes they motioned us to stand up and turn around. I immediately sensed what was afoot and dived off the road. Hell broke loose as I hit the ground. They seemed to open up with every weapon they had. After wriggling for about fifty yards without being hit I looked back and saw one of my section following me. At that moment his thigh was smashed by a heavy calibre bullet and blood splashed all around him. I turned back and made a tourniquet of some old flannelette but by the time I had finished he was unconscious either from loss of blood or pain. He was heavier than me and I could not drag him with me, so I had to leave him there. I continued to crawl towards the jungle but about that time the Norfolks opened fire on the Japanese and I managed to dodge both lots of fire and reached the Norfolk lines. After a short rest I set out and found my battalion headquarters and reported back.[21]

Ayer Hitam was the Loyals' last action on the mainland. It was clear by this time that Johore had been lost, and that night they were ordered to withdraw to Singapore island, where they arrived at 8.00 a.m. on 26 January. In fact, plans had been drawn up as early as 18 January for a final withdrawal to Singapore, although in order to preserve morale they were kept secret for the best part of a week. Now, however, as the prospect loomed of the entire Allied force being hemmed in at the southern tip of the peninsula, Percival issued the order for a phased withdrawal. The last week of January was spent trying to ensure that as many as possible made it back across the causeway linking the island to the mainland. The convergence of tens of thousands of Allied soldiers on Johore Bahru – the tip of the Malayan peninsula – presented a perfect bottleneck target for the Japanese, but Yamashita's supply lines were by now too extended to allow the rapid deployment of armoured divisions, and the wholesale demolition of bridges by the retreating Allies meant that there were few further losses. The last Allied troops to cross over to Singapore, at 7.30 a.m. on 31 January, were the Argyll and Sutherland Highlanders, accompanied by their two remaining pipers playing 'Hielan Laddie'; forty-five minutes later, sappers blew the causeway. All hope of a counter-offensive had vanished; the naval base was redundant; the battle for Malaya was lost, the siege of Singapore about to begin.

The little diamond-shaped island of Singapore – just twenty-seven miles from east to west and thirteen from north to south – was topographically not unlike Malaya: its coastline was indented with creeks, often enveloped by mangrove swamps, while much of its interior was gently undulating jungle. Its peacetime population was around three-quarters of a million, although by February 1942, swollen by refugees, at least a million were crammed in. Yet despite the fact that it was separated from the mainland by a channel 650 metres wide at its narrowest point – the Straits of Johore – its landward defences were pitifully inadequate, for it had always been assumed that any significant threat would be seaborne. Hence the construction of the great naval base at Sembawang, completed in 1938 at a cost of sixty million pounds.[22] Although situated on the north coast of the island, the fixed gun emplacements protecting it pointed seaward, and few of them could be redirected in time.[23] For the exhausted and demoralised Allied troops, therefore, the first week of February was spent constructing whatever field defences could be improvised – wire entanglements, trenches, earthworks, booby traps, minefields – while Japanese bombers overflew them almost unchallenged, making over a thousand sorties during the first two weeks of February and dropping nearly 800 tons of bombs.[24] On 5 February, the bombardment from Johore stepped up – a sure sign that invasion was imminent. What was not certain, however, was the direction from which it would come. Percival believed the Japanese would focus on the north-east of the island, but, as the warning signs intensified, several of his commanders became convinced that they would attack the north-west.

They were right. The invasion began around midnight on 8/9 February, with hundreds of small landing craft launching synchronised assaults on the north-west quarter of the island. Given the events of the past two months, Japanese expectations were high, but not even Yamashita can have anticipated such a rapid denouement. Within eighteen hours, despite desperate and costly resistance by the Australian troops assigned to this sector, his forces had established a foothold in the north-west; within two days, the causeway defence and naval base had been abandoned, as much as possible of the latter having first been blown up.

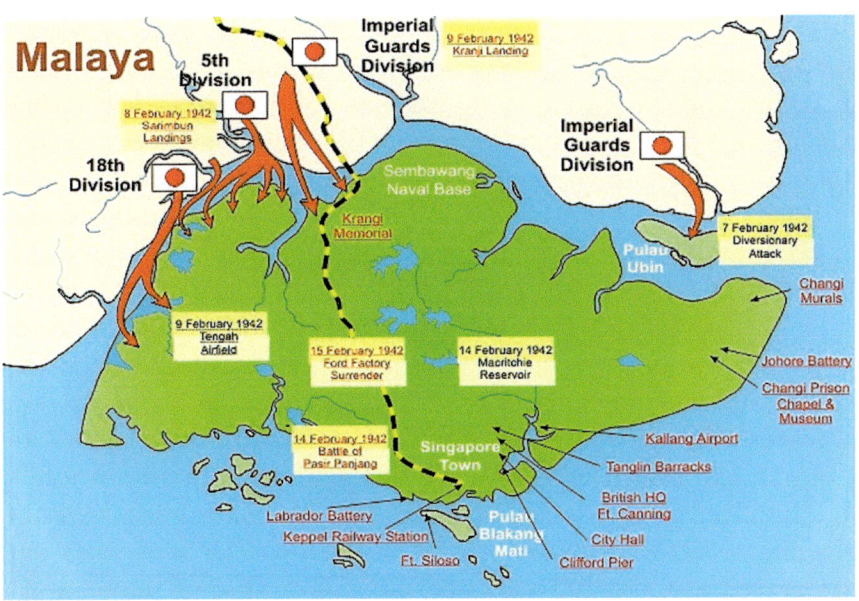

Singapore and the Japanese invasion

Within three days – by nightfall on 11 February – the Japanese had captured the high ground around Bukit Timah ('Tin Hill'), with its extensive food and fuel dumps, and were threatening the reservoirs which fed the city's water supply. That morning, Yamashita sent Percival a note demanding his surrender, but Percival ignored it. He had by now received a telegram from Churchill informing him that the battle for Singapore 'must be fought to the bitter end at all costs', with 'no thought of saving the troops or sparing the population' until after 'protracted fighting among the ruins of Singapore city' – for, as the prime minister put it, 'the whole reputation of our country and our race is involved'.[25] By the following morning, however, Percival had been obliged to order a withdrawal to an attenuated perimeter fringing the city itself.

Even this could not be held, and by 13 February the situation was critical: discipline was disintegrating, looters and deserters thronged the city, fuel and ammunition were running out and the water supply was about to be cut. The wharves at Keppel harbour were a scene of pandemonium, with thousands of soldiers and civilians trying to find a ship, a launch or even a *sampan* (rowing-boat) in which to get away. Others wandered sullenly about, discarding their weapons, foraging for food and refusing to return to their units. A number of Allied commanders now advocated surrender, but Percival still demurred: 'I have my honour to consider,' he protested. 'You lost that a long time ago in the north,' retorted Lt-General Sir Lewis Heath, commander of III Indian Corps, which two months earlier had borne the brunt of the initial onslaught at Jitra and Gurun.[26] Yet there were sectors of the perimeter which continued to be fiercely contested, among them the south-western corner, where the Loyals still defended the Pasir Panjang ridge. By the next day, however, this too had been lost, and the Loyals forced back to Gillman barracks, their home for so long in less taxing times. A few hundred yards ahead of them was the Alexandra Military Hospital, where, on the afternoon of the 14th, Japanese infantry massacred around 200 patients and staff, most of whom were bayoneted – an atrocity for which their commanders would later be held to account.

By daylight on Sunday 15 February, it was clear that the situation was hopeless. Few pockets of resistance were left, and those that remained were in desperate straits, as exemplified by Col. Elrington's account of the scene at Gillman barracks, where the Loyals were reduced to 289 men of all ranks:

> In addition to the incessant shelling and mortaring which by this time had reached crescendo, the aimed small-arms fire from the chalet spur and the road-junction just south of it was making things extremely difficult in the barrack area, particularly on the left flank across the open ground to the transport lines ... It is difficult to portray the grim activity of this critical last hour in Gillman barracks; so much happened in so little space. The zip-zipping and phut-phut of bullets from all angles, the bang-banging of mortars, the hiss and scream of shells, the blasting of brick and cracking cement; breathless runners with vital messages, the plop-plop of our own mortars under steady direction till their ammunition was done; the rush of a scared carrier crew, the sturdy stretcher-bearers, the hard-driven trucks with their mutilated loads, the set, determined faces of those ordered to cover the withdrawal and the unhurried walk of officers seeing to essentials; in short, the stir and stress of close combat in modern war, without loss of control.[27]

By mid-morning, Percival had finally conceded that he must surrender 'while Japanese soldiery could still be controlled by their commander'.[28] One and a half million bottles of spirits and 60,000 gallons of *samsu* (Chinese liquor) had been destroyed in the hope of forestalling a drunken victory rampage such as that inflicted on Nanjing four years earlier. Fortunately, Yamashita was equally aware of this danger. When he and Percival eventually sat down together at the Ford Motor Factory at Bukit Timah that afternoon, despite refusing to accept anything short of unconditional surrender, he promised protection for British civilians and allowed 1,000 Allied soldiers to be kept under arms overnight to preserve order. The following morning, when Japanese units advanced to claim their prize, he halted them on the outskirts of the city 'in consideration of possible outbreaks of disorders [*sic*] and inauspicious events'. Indeed, he never allowed most of his combat troops to enter the city, instead using military police and selected companies as the vanguard of his new order.[29] He could afford to be magnanimous: at the outset of the Malayan Campaign, he had been given a hundred days to capture the Lion City (Sanskrit: *Singa Pura*), and it had taken him just sixty-nine.

Part of a contemporary record of Loyals killed or missing when Singapore surrendered (LIM)

PRISONER STORIES

'James'

Among the 36,000 Japanese soldiers who gathered along the Straits of Johore during the first week of February 1942 was Lt Harumi Ochi, the 23-year-old commander of a platoon of machine-gunners, who later published two candid volumes recounting his memories of the Malayan Campaign. A self-confessed womanizer, Ochi had managed to indulge himself whenever time allowed. Three days of rest in Kuala Lumpur had afforded him the time to acquaint himself with an Indian girl 'with good hips', and he still carried the handkerchief given to him by a Eurasian girl called Asuta in Thailand. But by the time he reached Johore Bahru, two months of relentless campaigning had brought his weight down from seventy-two to fifty-five kilos and he was itching to get the job over with.

Lt Ochi was something of a free spirit. Behind Johore's Skudai creek, where his unit was posted, was a hill with a view across the straits to Singapore island. This was strictly out of bounds to the troops, but not only did he decide to climb it, he also took with him a British prisoner, 'James', an artillery lieutenant captured five days earlier. According to Ochi, James was a 'strange fish', but he had expressed an interest in learning more about the Japanese psyche and the two men struck up an improbable friendship. When they reached the summit of the hill and were discussing the impending invasion of the island, James suddenly said, 'Please take me across with you. Hide me on one of the landing craft. I want to witness the heroic Japanese onslaught at first hand.' 'What nonsense,' replied Ochi, 'You will only die. Do you want to die at the hands of your own people?' But James persisted: 'The Japanese die for their emperor, don't they?' 'That's a very difficult question,' replied Ochi. 'In England, how do you think of his majesty the king? Don't you British have the same feeling of divine duty to be loyal to the royal family?' And so their conversation went on, ranging from Asian inscrutability, to patriotic devotion, to the defences of Singapore island, until eventually Ochi declared, 'Maybe I *will* take you along into the battle for Singapore, but you must promise to keep it secret from the other soldiers.'

And so he did, remarkably. Lying in the darkness at the bottom of a landing craft, James was hidden from the surrounding dinghies, although the twenty or so men in Ochi's platoon knew he was there. Perhaps Ochi had told them that the British POW could provide them with information about the Allied defences. What became of 'James' is as uncertain as his identity. He may well have been killed in the assault. Ochi himself was wounded in the shoulder, though not seriously, and used the handkerchief given to him by Asuta to bandage the injury. Later, after Singapore fell, his unit was ordered to execute eleven Chinese suspected of anti-Japanese sympathies, but (according to his memoirs) he saw no reason to do so and disobeyed the order, releasing ten and committing one to temporary custody. Yet he continued after the war to maintain his belief that Japan had acted properly, waging war not simply to extend its own reach but in order to liberate the peoples of Asia from European domination. Moreover, as he noted bitterly, General Percival's life was spared when Singapore surrendered, but when Japan surrendered General Yamashita was hanged: 'Such is the white man's so-called humanism'.[30]

TWO

Fukai Maru

On 17 February 1942, the day after the occupation of Singapore city, the Japanese marched their British and Australian POWs some fifteen miles to the British military base at Changi on the north-eastern tip of the island (now the main airport). Built over the previous twenty years to provide a high standard of comfort for Singapore's imperial masters, Changi had theatres and cinemas, tennis courts, swimming pools and a yacht marina, all set within two square miles of lush hillocks, red hibiscus, white and magenta bougainvillea and palm-lined beaches, although heavy shelling during the previous two months had destroyed much of its infrastructure, including the water, power and sewage systems. Nor

Changi, the 'Malay Lines', where the Loyals were held (*IDS*)

had it been designed to house anything like the 50,000–60,000 men who were now herded into its four main barracks.

For the first month or two, the prisoners busied themselves with repairing the facilities and were free to move around more or less as they pleased. Most of the guard-duty was in the hands of Sikh 'renegades', as the British saw them (although in fact thousands of Indian soldiers refused to renounce their allegiance to the Empire, despite both bribes and torture). Allied officers were made responsible for the organisation and discipline of the camp. This was not simply because the Japanese were overwhelmed by the sheer number who had surrendered, but because their minds were elsewhere. Their first priority was to eliminate perceived anti-Japanese elements among the Chinese population of the island. Hence the *Sook Ching* ('purge through cleansing'), which began on 18 February and lasted two weeks, during which between 5,000 (the Japanese estimate) and 70,000 (the Chinese estimate) native Singaporeans, identified by hooded informers working for the *Kempeitai*, were driven to various locations around the island to be machine-gunned or bayoneted to death. Many of these massacres occurred on the beaches close to Changi, and parties of British and Australian POWs were sent out to retrieve corpses and bury them in mass graves.

Yet if such scenes served to remind the Allied POWs of the higher price paid by others who had fought alongside them, the accumulation of regulations and indignities soon dispelled any ambiguity about their status as prisoners. Singapore was re-named *Syonan-To* ('Light of the South Island') and clocks put forward an hour and a half to Tokyo time, which meant that reveille was usually held in darkness. The singing of national anthems was forbidden. From mid-March, prisoners were ordered to remain within their barracks' perimeters. Any who attempted to escape would be shot, and at least thirteen were. Officers were obliged to remove their badges of rank and simply attach one pip to their left breast pocket, and all ranks, officers included, were obliged to salute both Japanese and Indian sentries or, if they were not wearing caps, to 'bow deeply from the waist and remain thus until the guard had passed by'.[1] For many Allied prisoners, bowing was a humiliation that would never cease to rankle.

For the remaining three and a half years of the Pacific War, Changi continued to act as a home camp for Allied prisoners of war, the hub from which labouring parties numbering thousands were despatched throughout the 'Empire of Great Japan' (*Dai Nippon Teikoku*) as and when required, and to which many periodically returned. Numbers at Changi thus fluctuated greatly. By November 1942, only 11,000 prisoners remained; a month later the figure was back up to 26,300. By this time, many of them were being sent north to work on the Burma–Thailand railway, with some of their barracks converted into housing for the hundreds of young Korean women brought to Singapore to 'comfort' Japanese soldiery.

Those prisoners who survived and later returned to Changi regarded it as a haven, and many of them came to look back on those first few months as a time of innocence. It was during this deceptive prelude to the miseries which followed that the first five issues of *Nor Iron Bars* were produced, on 6 April, 16 April, 4 May, 6 June and 12 July 1942. Its aim was to provide 'humorous and topical articles' in order to alleviate boredom and 'occupy the minds of a few individuals' – that is to say, the thirty or so officers of the Loyals. Later issues would display a sharper edge, but those produced at Changi have a certain playfulness of tone, not so much foreboding as gratitude for being alive, although tempered with shame at what was seen as an enforced capitulation, best captured in a series of poems about 'Albert in Malaya' based on Marriott Edgar's 'Albert and the Lion' as immortalised by Stanley Holloway.

Searching for a diverting way to depict their plight, one contributor to the first issue also provided 'Archaeological Notes' on an imagined 'Expedition to the Orient' in the year 2053, after a great earthquake had rendered 'the Nipponese race' extinct. Led by 'Sir John Walker and Captain Haig', the excavation team found evidence of approximately 50,000 white men living in 'the small British colony of Syonan' under 'a most primitive form of civilization presumed to have been derived from their prehistoric ancestors'. As far as could be determined, their dress consisted of sarongs made from *atap* (palm-fronds) and bamboo sandals, and they ate very little apart from rice flavoured with local fruit

'Albert at Changi' (*NIB*, Christmas 1942)

and vegetables such as papaya, coconut or pineapple and the occasional morsel of pig or chicken. The discovery of mortars, pestles and 'grinding instruments of solid stone' reminiscent of the Palaeolithic age suggested that rice might also be crushed into flour to make bread. Their buildings were of stone or brick, two or three storeys high, attached to which were outhouses of *atap* containing iron buckets, the purpose of which was 'not exactly certain'. Skeletal analysis indicated that many had died of starvation.

In fact, few POWs died of starvation at Changi, although the vitamin-deficient rations led to a shocking 8,000 cases of dysentery during the first three months, and a good proportion of the 223 deaths during the same period were clearly the result of malnutrition. Beriberi (caused by vitamin B deficiency), dengue fever and malaria were also prevalent, exacerbated by the infestation of flies and mosquitoes.[2] In the second issue of *Nor Iron Bars*, one wag produced an illustration of 'one of the lesser known coats of arms', that of the Changi Rice-Grinders' Guild, whose motto was *Rice et Praeterea Nihil* ('rice and nothing else'). 'Never was so little waited for by so many for so long,' quipped one POW as he queued, mess-tin in hand, to receive his daily eight ounces of rice plus whatever titbits might be available.[3] There was also a tin of pineapple per prisoner, a personal gift from the occupant of the Imperial Chrysanthemum Throne – one tin in four months.

In July, when an order came down to provide 3,300 men to go to Japan, the Loyals were asked if they wished to go. This was not an easy decision, for it would almost certainly mean that they would remain incarcerated until the end of the war, however long that might be. On the other hand, the climate would be healthier than the relentless, sticky ninety-degree heat of Singapore, and after some discussion they voted in favour. Leaving Changi on 16 August, they were taken by truck to Keppel harbour, where, after a formalin bath on a Japanese fumigation ship, they were ordered aboard a 'dirty tramp steamer' of 3,800 tons called the *Fukai Maru*. A party of 400 engineers and senior officers – full colonels and above, including General Percival – was scheduled to accompany them, but after Percival protested at the conditions they were moved to another ship. Yet with 300 Australians already on board, the Loyals and others from Changi made a total of 1,100 POWs to cram into the *Fukai Maru*'s four holds. They were embarking on the most perilous five weeks of their captivity.

By May 1942, five months after Pearl Harbour, Japan had occupied Malaya, Singapore, Hong Kong, the Philippines (where close to 100,000 more Filipino and American prisoners were taken), Borneo, Burma, the Dutch East Indies, the Celebes, Solomon and Marianas islands, northern New Guinea and a host of smaller islands and territories. From Korea to Indochina, they controlled mainland Asia's eastern seaboard. The rapidity with which the western Pacific had been reinvented as a Japanese sea was a source of astonishment and jubilation. Prime Minister Tojo was hailed as a hero, news of each conquest celebrated as a vindication of Japan's manifest destiny. Access to oil, rubber and tin was guaranteed for the foreseeable future. The 'Greater East Asian Co-Prosperity Sphere' (*Dai Toa Kyoeiken*) which Japan had been advocating for years was a reality, and a seemingly defensible perimeter created against the threat of counter-attack. In order to defend this perimeter, however, Japan needed constantly to move its troops, supplies and captive labour force to wherever its empire needed them, and for the most part this had to be done by sea. Command of the shipping lanes was thus crucial, but therein lay the danger, for by May 1942 American cryptographers had managed to infiltrate Japan's naval codes. Admiral Nimitz, commander in chief of the United States Pacific Fleet, was thus aware almost from its inception of Admiral Yamamoto's plan to lure him into a trap at Midway, a Pacific atoll equidistant from Asia and America, and instead it was Nimitz who laid an ambush for Yamamoto. The resulting battle of Midway (4–7 June) was a Japanese disaster. Four of its aircraft carriers and one heavy cruiser were sunk; the United States lost one aircraft carrier and one destroyer. It was the first major defeat that Japan had suffered, the first – and arguably the decisive – turning point of the Pacific War. For Allied prisoners, however, it was a double-edged sword. The Japanese did not mark ships carrying prisoners of war, so that neither American aircraft nor their submarine wolfpacks, now increasingly free to carry out search and destroy missions in the western Pacific, had any means of distinguishing them from troopships or supply vessels. Approximately two in five of the 50,000 prisoners transported by ship around Japan's empire between 1942 and 1945 perished at sea, many of them killed by friendly fire. Most of the others died because of the conditions they endured aboard the 'hellships' in which they were carried.[4]

One of these hellships was the *Fukai Maru*. Each of its four upper holds had to accommodate between 185 and 365 POWs in a space between twenty and thirty yards long and fifteen yards wide. Two tiers of rudimentary shelving had been constructed for them to lie on, but each shelf was just nine feet long, seven feet wide and less than five feet high, and had to sleep fifteen

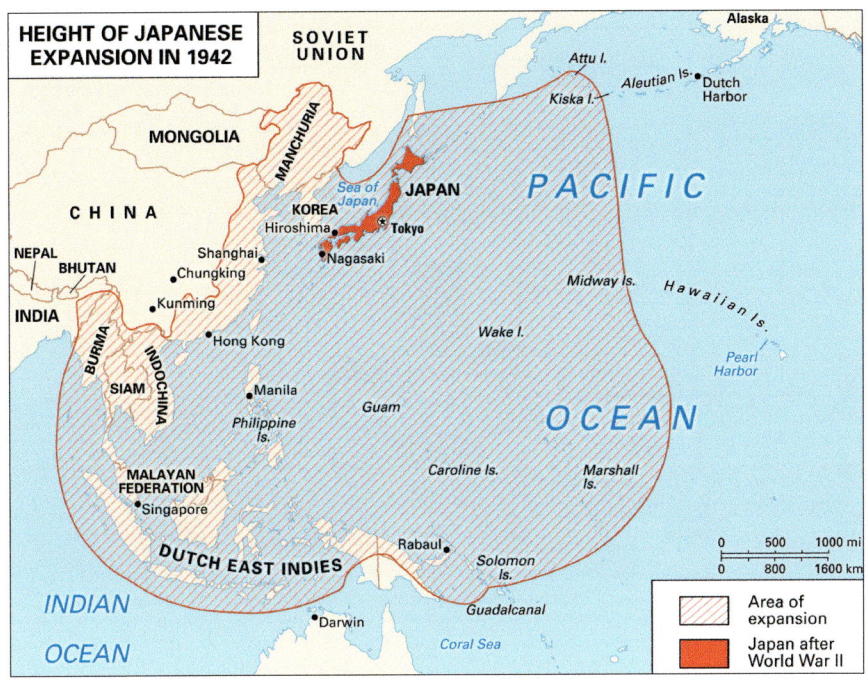

The limits of Japan's empire, 1942

men. This left six feet by two feet per man, plus his kitbag. Under him was a thin layer of straw matting infested with rats, lice and cockroaches. Each hold-load of prisoners was allowed on deck for six hours a day, but the remaining eighteen hours had to be spent in the steel-hulled, poorly ventilated, stiflingly hot holds. In rough weather, when the hatches were closed, the air was 'thick and foul' from the retching caused by the rolling and tossing of the ship. Wooden latrines had been constructed on deck, overhanging the ship's side, but there were only three per 200 men, most of whom were suffering from diarrhoea. According to one POW, the safest thing to do was to follow each visit by returning straight to the end of the queue.[5]

There were also cooking facilities on deck, but only 'of the most primitive nature', and the daily allowance was utterly inadequate: two cups of rice and barley in a ratio of two to one, one cup of watery stew flavoured with cabbage or onion, and one fifth of a tin

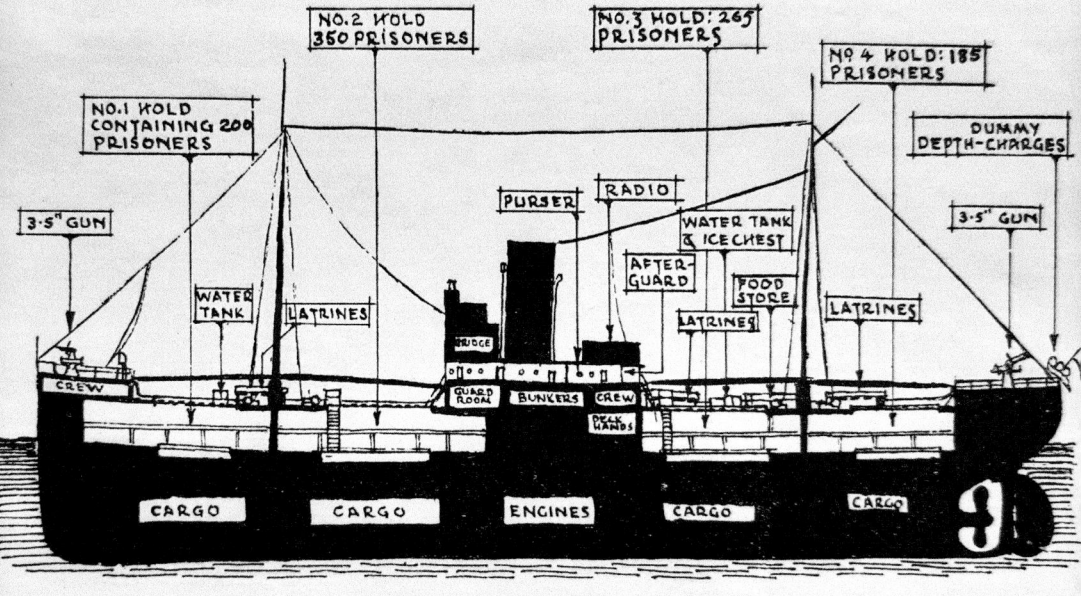

Sectional view of the *Fukai Maru* (*IDS*)

of indeterminate meat and vegetable.[6] Desperate with hunger, men on deck clustered around the galley, where the quartermaster had to mount a permanent watch to stop them breaking in, not always to good effect: one group of prisoners set up the 'onion racket', which involved a man climbing over the side of the ship, kicking his way into the vegetable store and passing onions to waiting comrades. When the Japanese guards discovered this, the culprit was made to stand on the bridge for four hours holding three large onions in each outstretched hand.[7]

On 29 August, ten days out from Singapore, the *Fukai Maru* reached Takao on Formosa (Taiwan), where it docked for over two weeks while the POWs loaded and unloaded bauxite, coal and rice. Although the intake of rice did not lead to any increase in their on-board rations, at least those who volunteered for this 'coolie duty' received three meals a day, while those who remained on board were able to trade articles of woollen clothing for bananas and sweetmeats. Working parties were also ferried ashore for heavy lifting in the coal yard or the oil depot, where one Australian corporal claimed with satisfaction to have sabotaged a number of Japanese motor torpedo boats which were in for repairs. One of the Loyals' officers who went ashore was the diarist John Lever, who recorded his conversation with a group of smartly-dressed Japanese on the quayside. 'What do you think of the war between Britain and Japan?' he was asked. 'I think Britain will win eventually,' replied Lever. Ridiculous, said the Japanese. And what about the war between Russia and Germany? Lever replied that he thought Russia would win. 'Oh no, Russia has practically lost. Stalingrad will fall any day now,' said the Japanese.

Punishment when the 'onion racket' was discovered (*IDS*)

However, he evidently had more respect for the Russians than for the British, 'because they are not really European, they are more Asian, so they could not easily be beaten'.[8]

Before leaving Formosa on the morning of 15 September, rumours were heard about typhoons and 'terrible deep-sea monsters that might sink us without warning'. By the time they passed the Pescadores Islands that evening, the warnings had become more insistent: according to local fishermen, a great sea-serpent with star-like eyes and stripes down its body was attacking all the shipping in the vicinity.[9] This self-evident code for an American submarine persuaded the commander to turn back to port, but the following evening he set out again, accompanied by escort vessels. Yet Japan was no longer the *Fukai Maru*'s destination; instead, they were heading for Korea (or 'Chosen' as

Below decks on the *Fukai Maru* (*IDS*)

the Japanese called it). No reason was given for the change of plan, but the prisoners noticed that the ship now began to zig-zag.

As they steamed north, the weather grew colder, and those who had traded their woollens for food in Takao began to regret it. With the typhoon season approaching, the sea was also rougher. The outrigged latrines on deck were swept away in a storm, sanitary conditions deteriorated, and increasing numbers succumbed to disease: two men with diphtheria had had to be left behind at Takao and more than half the POWs were now suffering from scurvy, dysentery or an unidentified 'plague'. Luckily the journey to Busan on the south coast of Korea only took a week, and although there were no deaths on board, the prisoners arrived so weak with hunger that about twenty had to be taken straight to the local military hospital. Seven of the Loyals died within the next six weeks. Most of them had acute dysentery and one had beriberi.

On 24 September, two days after arriving, the prisoners disembarked and were told that before moving on by train they must first meet their hosts. It was thirty years since the Japanese had annexed Korea, and the chance to exhibit their spoils of war to the native population was too good to miss. It was, after all, for the liberation of East Asia from western imperialism that Japan had gone to war, and nothing constituted more tangible proof of its new order than a thousand captive imperialists. Despite the fact that Busan railway station was less than a mile from the dock, the prisoners were therefore obliged to march five miles around the town 'to give the inhabitants a treat'. A public holiday was announced and 120,000 Koreans were called out to see them, many in brightly-coloured national dress, but, according to 'Albert', 'the natives just stared at them daft-like, as though they was summat from t'zoo'.

At least the train, when they eventually boarded it, was not a disappointment. Expecting cattle trucks, they were pleasantly surprised to be seated in 'very comfortable' carriages, while the rations – two boxes for each man, one containing rice, the other 'tasty bits of meat and fish', plus a pair of chopsticks – were 'extraordinarily good after the food on the ship'.[10] It was thus a marginally revived party of 460 men who arrived the next day at

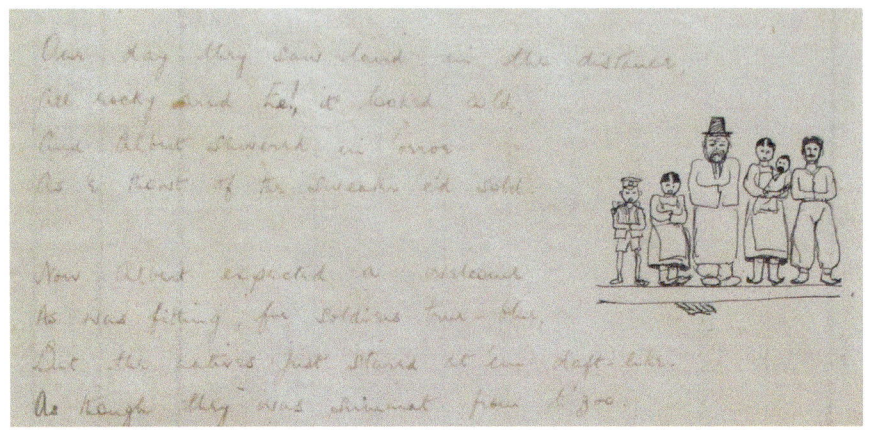

Koreans staring at Allied POWs, from 'Albert's Odyssey', *NIB* Christmas 1942

Keijo (the rest having been taken on to the branch camp at Jinsen (Incheon), about fifteen miles away) and, after once again being paraded through the streets, were escorted into the 'grey and forbidding' former silk-reeling mill which, for the next three years, many of them would be obliged to call home.

On 1 October 1942, nine days after the *Fukai Maru* docked at Busan, the hellship *Lisbon Maru* was torpedoed by *USS Grouper*, an American submarine scouring the East China Sea. *Lisbon Maru* was carrying 700 Japanese army personnel and – unknown to the commander of the *Grouper* – 1,816 British and Canadian POWs captured at Hong Kong. As on the *Fukai Maru*, they were packed into the ship's holds in atrocious conditions. When the torpedo struck, the Japanese evacuated the ship, but only after battening down the hatches to the holds. Realizing that the ship was sinking, some prisoners managed to break open their hatches and jump overboard. British accounts claimed that Japanese guards initially began firing at them in the water, but this was refuted by the Japanese. Whatever the truth, the upshot was that 846 POWs lost their lives, most of them in the holds, some in the water, although almost 1,000 of them were saved by either Japanese escort boats or Chinese fishermen.

Two weeks later, when news of the tragedy reached Keijo, the camp commander Col. Noguchi invited the POWs to write down for him their impressions of their journey from Singapore.[11] What they composed for his eyes has not survived, but when the January 1943 issue of *Nor Iron Bars* appeared, memories of the *Fukai Maru* and the fractions of fortune by which they had escaped the fate of the *Lisbon Maru* were still raw. Poignant and seething with anger, the prisoners' contributions are epitomized by a poem 'To the Survivors of the *Lisbon Maru*'.

> When we heard of the fate of your prison
> And the men who were said to be drowned,
> We remembered how often we wondered
> If we should arrive safe and sound.
> For many a doubt had arisen
> If we should emerge to the light,
> Should some Yankee commander have blundered
> And torpedoed us during the night.
> We wondered just how you were faring
> At the time the disaster occurred.
> Were you feeding, as we were, on nothing
> But rice and the smell of a curd?
> Was your 'Jamban'[12] past all human bearing
> With a stink rising up to the skies,
> Using one hand to hold up your clothing,
> With the other dispersing the flies?
> Were you herded together like cattle,
> Forty-four cubic feet to a man,
> With the roof about three feet or under
> And just turn around if you can?
> With no air and a regular battle
> For light down below at the back,
> While the boots up above seemed to thunder
> And lice and dirt dropped through the crack?
> But why should I go on detailing
> The horrors and shame of the ship?
> A reckoning will come, never doubt it,
> And then we'll remember that trip.
> Then let there be weeping and wailing,
> And see that you make it worthwhile.
> Yes, then let us all set about it,
> And it won't be the Nips' turn to smile!

Yet the havoc now being wreaked on Japanese shipping also brought hope. One of the reasons why construction began on the Burma–Thailand railway in October 1942 was because the sea routes were becoming risky. The Pacific War was at a crossroads.

PRISONER STORIES

Gunner Starkey

Having disembarked the Loyals at Busan in September 1942, the *Fukai Maru* continued for two years to ferry troops, supplies and POWs around the Western Pacific. Its last voyage left Manila on 20 September 1944, bound for Formosa. One of the POWs on board was Gunner L. F. Starkey of the 125th Tank Regiment, Royal Artillery:[13]

> We sailed due north all that day but as soon as darkness fell the convoy dropped anchor and holed up for the night amongst the islands just north of Luzon, the largest island in the Philippines, so we waited there until daylight, when we set sail again as before going due north. The only difference which I noticed was the number on our funnel which indicated the position of our ship in the convoy. On 20 September we were number 5 but on 21 September we were now number 2 which got me wondering.
>
> It was a lovely summer's day with clear, blue skies as we sailed along but around 9 a.m. the air raid alarm was sounded and we were all herded below to what eventually turned out to be an experience I will never forget. As the ack-ack guns were blazing above decks we were all sat below hoping that we were going to survive an attack on this convoy – oddly enough being carried out by our friends and allies, the USA Naval Air Force. After approximately two minutes of the attack, which seemed an eternity, there was a sickening thud followed by a vivid flash and a terrifying explosion. Within seconds the hold below us was full of water and those who were on this deck were swimming around looking for a way out. Seeing this, I thought it was time I should be getting off.
>
> The main way out to the top deck originally was a wooden staircase in the centre of the hold but with the explosion, this had vanished into the water in the hold below. That left the only exit being an iron-runged ladder in the corner farthest

away from me. As I looked across, I saw a crowd of the lads around climbing the same and by this time water was coming into our hold. I was beginning to think this was the end. What a way to go after surviving all the suffering of the past two and a half years.

What happened to me during the next two minutes only God knows because I can't remember leaving my bed space. The only thing I remember was being half way up the ladder with the hold still crowded. It seems that I must have walked over their heads. It was amazing and I still often sit and think and wonder how I got there.

When I arrived out on the deck the ship was very low in the water. I had to wade through water to the rail as the deck was now awash so I had to act quickly but having learned to swim six months previously, I was able to cope with the perils that faced me but as I waited a few more seconds my eyes looked to the skies that were filled with planes, one of them diving towards our stricken ship and dropping a torpedo into the sea which was speeding our way. I was transfixed, waiting for the thud which never came as the dreaded monster carried on then exploded into the side of another ship astern of us.

With the decision now made I took the plunge from the rails into the sea and to the best of my ability began to get as much distance as I could between me and the stricken ship. After completing about twenty yards I looked back to see the *Fukai Maru* slide to a watery grave, stern first. It was a sight that will linger with me to my grave. The only regret I have about this episode is the grief I feel for the 1,000 fellow POWs that now lay with her at the bottom of the South China Sea.

When all the hullabaloo had died down I looked to find any of the wreckage which would help me to keep afloat a little longer, so I collected some bits of wood and made a little raft whereupon I was joined by a friend, Joe Wilbur from the 88th Anti-Tank Regiment and he became my partner for the next few hours. Between us we tried to paddle our little raft towards a small island we could see in the distance but as the hours went by we seemed to be getting no nearer and we were both in a sorry state. By now I was suffering from sickness and diarrhoea and with being practically naked I was shivering with cold as it was now 4 p.m. and we had now been in the water for seven hours. Just about this time, when all seemed lost, some small Japanese fishing boats came around picking up any survivors and, from a distance of approximately forty yards, one called out to us to swim out to it to be picked up. The way I was feeling I didn't think I would be able to make it so I told Joe Wilbur to go and leave me and when he was on board they would probably come closer to pick me up. I watched him swim to the boat and be pulled aboard. I was glad for him but a further shock was in store for me because shortly afterwards they set off and sailed out of sight.

This I thought was the end for me and I began to wish I had tried to swim to the ship and, if I did not make it, better to die making an attempt than die without. Once again I had to set about trying to get to the island I could see but the more I paddled the further I seemed to be going away. The tide was going the wrong way.

By now it was becoming dusk and I was wondering just how much longer I could last. My thoughts drifted towards home and oh, how I longed to be there at that moment but again lady luck was with me. Another small fishing boat appeared out of the gloom and I was beckoned to swim to it. This time regardless of the distance I set off to swim towards my saviours and reached the smack. I was very tired and sick and when I was pulled aboard (please forgive me all you FEPOWs), I never thanked a Japanese person so much in all my life and meant every word. I was so grateful for being saved.

Taken back to Manila, Starkey was placed in Bilibid prison where he remained until liberated by United States troops on 5 February 1945.

THREE

Endurance

BEFORE INSPECTING THEIR QUARTERS, the 460 POWs who arrived at Keijo on 25 September 1942 were lined up on the exercise yard and formally welcomed by the camp commander, Col. Yuzuru Noguchi, a 57-year-old military careerist with over thirty years of service in the Imperial Army. A short man even by Japanese standards, with a toothbrush moustache and a receding hairline, Noguchi liked to stand on a podium at some distance from his 'guests' while addressing them. He clearly enjoyed lecturing them, often 'at considerable length and with considerable irrelevance', and subsequent issues of *Nor Iron Bars* included pastiches of his speeches, of which his interpreter circulated tortured English translations.[1] Yet compared to many Japanese camp commanders, he was not an unreasonable man, although he was a stickler for protocol. Requests were considered only if presented to him in person by either the senior Allied officer, Col. Elrington, or his adjutant, Capt. 'Jiminy' Paque, and disrespect or levity were strictly prohibited: one of his orders banned use of the terms 'Nips' or 'Japs'.

Noguchi began by introducing himself as 'Superintendent of the Chosen [Korea] War Prisoners' Camp' – comprising Keijo and its branch camps at Jinsen (Incheon) and, later, Konan (Hungnan). This war, he said, was not of Japan's making. It was America and Britain that had 'overwhelmed Nippon, the important defenser [*sic*] of Asia, to the extent that they dared to resort to violence of economic disruption', creating chaos in China and threatening 'the very existence of our nation'. Yet 'Heaven is always on the side of Justice', and although the POWs had fought bravely, they now faced the reality of defeat: 'I think these war results

Col. Noguchi welcoming the POWs to Keijo Camp (*IDS*)

do not signify the inferior power of our enemy but rather owe to our absolute indomitable power protected by *Kami* (Heaven). Wherever Nippon Army and Navy advance, *Tenyu Shinjo* (Special Providential Help) always follow. You should recognize the fact and consider the reasons. Nippon Army and Navy are under the Imperial Command of *Tenno* (Emperor) who is the personification of *Kami*, so that the Imperial troops are to be called the Troops of God. You have become war prisoners because of struggling against *Kami-no-Gun* (God's Army), and now you are convinced of fearfulness to the marrow and become aware of unsavoury results. What do you think of this?'

This being a rhetorical question, Noguchi proceeded to answer it. 'Some of you will hold hostile feeling against us in your hearts; that can never be permission. We will punish you if you act against our regulations, for instance disobedience, resistance and escape, even attempt to do so, are understood as manifestation of hostility. You should reflect on yourselves.' Limits would be placed on their freedom. Those who continued to harbour malice in their hearts would be placed under additional restraint 'and must endure pain in compensation of hostility'. Regulations for daily life in the camp would be issued, and every POW must obey them. 'Prejudice against labour and grumbling over food, clothing and housing are strictly prohibited. Closing my instruction, I advise you all to find interest and anxiety in your forthcoming daily life by acting according to the Imperial military discipline. You have not come here as honoured guests. You must endure.'[2]

Before dismissing them, Noguchi announced that they must all sign a declaration promising not to try to escape, on pain of death. When Col. Elrington replied that they could not do this, he was told that they would remain there without food until they did. Two hours later, faint with hunger and following Elrington's reassurance that they were only signing under duress, the POWs eventually agreed. Before falling out they were also introduced to Noguchi's principal assistants: Capt. Isamu Goto, second-in-command; Lt Takeo Terada, adjutant; Lt Katawani, the paymaster; and Capt. Goro Uchida, a civilian doctor who had served briefly in the army in 1935–6 and was now drafted in as senior medical orderly at Keijo. It was the knuckle-happy Lt Terada, the senior on-site guard, whom the POWs would especially come to fear.

The main camp building, the former silk-reeling mill, was of brick construction, approximately thirty metres by twenty, set in a 'rather slummy district' of Keijo but enjoying a decent view of the mountains that ringed the city. The fifty or so officers were allocated the top floor as their mess, with about six square feet of a long wooden bench per man, a thin straw mat (*tatami*) to sleep on and a shelf for their kit. Only Col. Elrington was allowed a camp-bed, although other senior officers were allowed to construct individual cubicles. The 400 other ranks used the squad-rooms on the second and third floors, where they slept head to toe on benches with about six by two and a half feet per man, much the same as on the *Fukai Maru* but with unrestricted headroom. Everyone received five or six blankets (depending on age) and each squad-room contained one inadequate stove which was only lit for three months each winter, despite the intense cold. The rooms were poorly lit, with narrow windows admitting little light and feeble bulbs which could only be switched on at certain times. To read, a man needed to be near a window, but if he stood too close he blocked the light for others. The ground floor was communal space, part of which was converted into a makeshift concert room with a small stage at one end. There was also a canteen, where POWs were told they could buy extra supplies, but most of the time it was 'just an empty shed with canteen written over the door'. The compound, which was surrounded by a wooden fence topped with barbed-wire and punctuated by sentry-boxes, contained an office, guardhouse and isolation cells, cookhouse, wash-house, latrine block (*benjo*), garage, fuel store, married and unmarried guards' quarters and a gravelly, pot-holed exercise yard about sixty by eighty metres. The wash-house had two large communal bath-tubs where each man was permitted two hot baths per week, five to a tub. As for the *benjos*, they were

Keijo Camp, interior and exterior views (*IDS*)

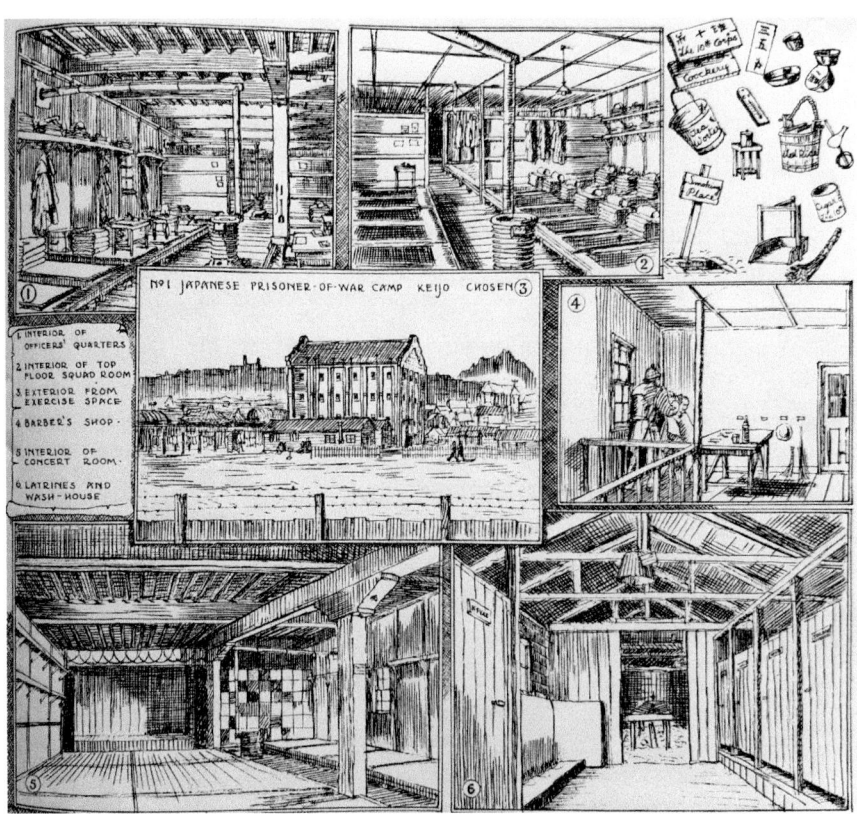

'just a hole in the floor', the pits below which were emptied each week by Korean peasants to fertilize their fields. Everything at Keijo was bare, squalid and unwelcoming.

It took no more than a day or two for the POWs' life to settle into a leaden routine of familiar irritations, the first of which was their hosts' insistence that they learn to salute and bow in Japanese fashion. Saluting with the palm of the hand facing downward was not too difficult to master, but bowing stiffly to an angle of precisely fifteen degrees necessitated a series of 'bowing parades' with Lt Terada. 'More,' cried Terada after their first attempt: they must bend further, and from the hip. 'More, more!' 'And now,' he announced when they eventually got the hang of it, 'we will have bowing on the march'. But why, wrote John Lever, must the Japanese do this 'grovelling salute-cum-bow which we all dislike so?' The answer lay deeply ingrained in Japanese etiquette. The origins of bowing (*ojigi*) lay in the Samurai values of respect, rank and 'face'. The victors had earned that respect. The vanquished had forfeited it, and must acknowledge the fact. But the prisoners did at least record one minor victory: when Terada told them to march in the high-stepping, foot-stomping Japanese goose-step style, they acquitted themselves so shambolically that he soon gave up. They could march as they wished, he told them, as long as they promised to do so smartly when outside the camp.[3]

Every day began with reveille, 'a Boy Scout bugle-call' sounded at 5.30 in

Caricature of Japanese marching (*NIB*)

Every day began with a bugle-call (*NIB*)

midsummer and 7.00 in midwinter, followed a few minutes later by the first roll-call (*tenko*) of the day. Any prisoner who was not already standing to attention on his bed with his blankets folded, any squad-room leader who had not counted his men, the sick along with the healthy, before the duty officer and his adjutant marched through the door, was liable to be slapped. After the first week, moreover, *tenko* was conducted entirely in Japanese, and any man who called out his number (*bango*) incorrectly might also be slapped. Contributors to *Nor Iron Bars* helpfully provided lists of both Japanese numbers and English homonyms to help remember them, for 'Rites peculiar such as these/Are sacred to the Japanese'. An hour before lights out, at 8.00 or 8.30, the charade was repeated. The POWs hated it, and never ceased to do so.[4]

Less regular but also less predictable were the inspections and searches to which all ranks, their kit and their squad-rooms were periodically subjected. Some of these were announced in advance, such as the succession of visits during the early months of 1943 of an Imperial Army general, a delegation of military auditors, and a government officer from Tokyo, when it was not so much the POWs as Col. Noguchi and his staff who were being inspected.[5] Others were designed to catch the prisoners unaware, whether it was smoking more than three feet from an ashtray (strictly prohibited on account of the Japanese horror of fire) or gambling on card games (which, after one pack of cards was confiscated, was calculated mentally).[6] Since each squad-room always posted at least one lookout who called 'Red Light!' if a sentry approached, few prisoners were caught red-handed, but this seldom left time for the rooms to be tidied; during one surprise inspection in April 1943, the Japanese duty officer threatened to slap all the officers' faces if their mess-room was not cleaned up before the next roll-call. And when kitbags were searched, all sorts of things turned up: a private electric stove which one officer managed to conceal for several months was eventually confiscated in October 1944. The best excuse to offer if found with some unaccountable item was to say 'it came from Singapore', which apparently 'nearly

Roll-call, with Japanese numbering (*IDS*)

always worked even in the most ridiculous cases'. In addition to the periodic squad-room inspections, everyone who went out on a working-party also had to undergo *Searchu* twice a day: before leaving the camp (in case he was carrying anything which might be bartered with friendly Koreans) and when he returned (for evidence of either bartering or pilfering). This 'customary fingular [*sic*] prowl amongst pockets, socks and gussets' even led on one occasion to the confiscation of a private's penny whistle, although he swore blind that he had brought it from Singapore.[7]

It was not just contraband – however defined – that the guards were looking for. Reading material of any kind was meant to be

Squad-room inspection, with improbable explanations (*NIB*)

vetted by the camp interpreter, although since the POWs soon learned to copy his red stamp and the guards had practically no English, a good deal seems to have slipped through. Anything written by the POWs themselves was similarly suspect. Had *Nor Iron Bars* been discovered, there would certainly have been trouble; the fact that it was not is testimony to the care taken by the POWs to secrete it, as the editors regularly reminded them to do. When the YMCA sent a gramophone and a number of seventy-eight RPM records in late 1944, these too had to be vetted. How much even the interpreter understood of the American ragtime and big band lyrics so popular at the time was a matter for entertaining speculation: according to John Lever, by the time the records were

Vetting the gramophone records (*NIB*)

eventually passed on to the POWs, 'they had been censored so thoroughly a lot were worn out'.[8]

If the prisoners complained, they were told 'You must endure', a supposedly encouraging response which soon acquired the status of a mantra:

> Though days of peace are far behind, they'll come again – so never mind!
> Forget the present, fraught with pain, remember that you'll live again.
>
> You must endure!
>
> Your day's routine you may deplore, the early rising you abhor,
> You hate that bugle's strident note, twice-daily roll-calls get your goat.
>
> You must endure!
>
> Some mornings you will madly rush to eat your breakfast, do your wash,
> In time to fall in with your squad. You're off to warehouse – oh my God!
>
> You must endure!
>
> When in the afternoon you leave the heated room, don't over-grieve,
> As to the square you make your way to frolic[9] in the Nippon way.
>
> You must endure!
>
> A word of counsel for your ear: a little longer you must bear.
> Remember this! Let none dispute, the other foot shall wear the boot.
>
> Till then, endure!

All these were irritations, but more genuinely distressing was the rule that all incoming and outgoing mail had to pass through the censor's office, which meant long delays in both directions. Even in war-time, it usually did not take more than 3 to 6 months for letters to pass between Britain and East Asia, but it was over a year before the families of most POWs captured at Singapore received confirmation that their sons, siblings or fathers had been taken prisoner rather than killed, and it was not until August 1943 that the POWs at Keijo received their first letters from home. Any information which have might been considered useful (geographical, meteorological) or subversive (military or political) had naturally been cut out. When a second batch of letters arrived in January 1944, much of it was dated 1942. Sometimes these delays were deliberate: when Anthony Eden, the British Foreign Minister, criticised Japan's treatment of its POWs in the House of Commons in March 1944, Col. Noguchi retaliated by withholding all mail for several weeks.[10] In theory, the prisoners were allowed to write four postcards home each year, but anything that might be interpreted as criticism of the conditions in which they were held was also either cut out or struck through – even the fact that they were keeping a few pigs and rabbits in the camp, in case this implied that they were not being fed properly.

Which, of course, they were not. As in all Japanese camps, from the first day to the last, the prisoners' overriding obsession was food, always food. During their first year or so of captivity, the rations given to the POWs at Keijo were meagre and monotonous but not life-threateningly inadequate: breakfast was boiled rice ('gruel') and about a pint of vegetable stew, usually cabbage or *daikon* (white radish); lunch, a 200-gram loaf of bread, another pint of vegetable stew and about 55 grams (a sixth of a tin) of bully beef; supper, boiled rice and either vegetable or soya bean stew, sometimes flavoured with a few morsels of meat or fish. The bread was baked outside the camp and was 'soggy and virtually inedible' unless dried out on a stove, the fish was 'heads and tails', and the 'gruel' provoked repeated outbreaks of diarrhoea. In the opinion of one prisoner,

> Our practice is to use manure
> To make the growth of plants more sure.
> The Japs save time and trouble too
> By putting it straight in the stew.[11]

More importantly, the daily calorific value of this diet was only about 1,800, little more than half of what was needed for young men doing physical labour, and their average bodyweight loss was about fifteen per cent.

From the spring of 1943, as Japan came under increasing pressure, rations decreased. By the end of March, shortage of flour had brought a halt to the issue of bread (instead, they received more of 'the eternal, infernal rice') and bully was restricted to those who went out on working-parties.¹² Every month the prisoners were weighed, and throughout 1943 and most of 1944 their weight continued to fall. Only in November 1943, in anticipation of a Red Cross inspection, was a slight increase recorded, but by March 1944 this had been lost again. When Elrington complained to Noguchi, he was told that Europeans consumed far more than they needed to and there was a deficit in the mess account. By Japanese standards, Noguchi was right: the POWs themselves reckoned that the food they were given was comparable in both quantity and quality to what the Japanese guards got, and better than most of the 'dirt poor' Koreans among whom

Starving Korean trying to break into the camp (*NIB*)

they lived. Starving Koreans sometimes even tried to break into the camp, hoping to scrounge a few scraps.[13]

Nevertheless, Noguchi did make a few marginal concessions: from August 1943 flour re-appeared and was now given directly to the camp cooks (fellow prisoners) to bake bread for lunch – 'a vast improvement'. There were also weekly supplies of apples in the autumn, three-quarters of a pound of sugar per man every ten days, and some butter ('just a spot of grease'). Yet the daily staples continued to be reduced: by late 1944, the combined rice and bread ration was down to 410 grams a day and bits of meat and fish only featured in the stew about twice a month, usually replaced by seaweed. The prisoners were now getting less than 1,500 calories a day and their bodyweight loss averaged between twenty and twenty-five percent. John Lever, whose pre-war weight was around eighty kilos, now weighed just sixty-one.[14]

Such paucity required meticulous measures for ensuring the distribution of equal shares. Although they ate in their mess-rooms, it was in the cookhouse that the food was prepared, and only nominated mess-orderlies were allowed to collect it and bring it to the rooms, where a queue would already have formed. A mildly satirical but all too believable article entitled 'Meal-Time Memoranda' in *Nor Iron Bars* listed the different forms of queuing behaviour and what they revealed of the men's characters. There was 'the impatient man', always the first to arrive; 'the nervous man', constantly hopping about and peering to the front to make sure there was enough left; 'the hopeful man', who arrived with two bowls; 'the jealous man', who tiptoed around peering into each bowl to make sure no-one else got more than he did; 'the thrifty man', who would save some of his portion for later; 'the civilised man', who sat at a table and ceremoniously laid out his bowl and spoon before starting to eat; and finally 'the crafty man', who hung back until there was nothing left, then went around soliciting a contribution from everyone until he ended up with the largest portion.[15] Similar care was taken in divvying up the 340-gram tins of bully beef, but the nature of the product meant that this was easier said than done, so it was agreed that the mess-orderly would mentally number each sixth and then ask the

Speculating whether the 'sixth' system would catch on after the war (*NIB*)

men to choose a number from one to six. That way, if he had cut unequal pieces, he would be absolved of favouritism.[16]

The one day in the year when every POW was assured of a good meal was Christmas, for although Christmas was not a Japanese national holiday, their traditional reverence for festivals meant that even in the grimmest camps the POWs were almost invariably treated to a *yasume* (holiday) and extra rations on Christmas Day. For Christmas lunch at Keijo in 1942, there was tinned Irish stew, lettuce, potato salad and an apple per man. For those who could afford it, a selection of more exotic items was available for purchase in the canteen, including pilchards, sausage, Hokkaido butter, ham, marmalade, cans of pineapple, even beer, saki and white wine. This was followed by a concert put on by the officers, which the Japanese filmed and apparently enjoyed as much as the POWs. They even supplied 'some good lighting effects', although they had insisted on vetting the script beforehand. 'Christmas was always a good day,' wrote Henling Wade. 'It was the other 364 days that were hell.'[17] And as the war progressed and Japan's resources and supply-lines were increasingly disrupted, hope of improvement steadily receded.

Beginning in January 1943, one thin shaft of sunlight periodically broke through the monotonous gloom: the arrival of a consignment of Red Cross parcels. The POWs' first encounter with the International Committee of the Red Cross (ICRC) had not been encouraging. Anticipated with a flutter of expectation, it eventually took place on 18 December 1942, when Dr Fritz Paravicini, an 'apple-cheeked, shining' Swiss national, arrived at Keijo. According to Lever, he turned out to be 'a bitter disappointment'. Having travelled 400 miles to be there, Dr Paravicini spent just fourteen minutes going around the camp, accompanied throughout by a posse of Japanese officers, and did not speak to a single prisoner. After the war, Henling Wade discovered that the doctor had lived in Japan for thirty years, was married to a Japanese citizen and that 'his business depended upon Japanese goodwill'. Two years later, when news of Paravicini's death was posted in another camp he had inspected, the POWs are said to have greeted the news with cheers.[18]

Yet if Dr Paravicini seems to have been an unfortunate choice, his visit to Keijo was not unproductive, for shortly after Christmas the first ICRC consignment of parcels arrived. Three more would follow: in August 1943, January 1944 and November 1944. Dispatched from Britain, South Africa or the United States, they contained the sort of treats that POW dreams were made of: margarine, biscuits, syrup, galantine, bacon, sugar, apple pudding, prunes, tins of fish, bully beef or vegetables, tea, coffee, orange juice, tomatoes, creamed rice, cheese, chocolate, Nestlé milk powder, cocoa, toothpaste and soap and Chesterfield cigarettes. The parcels were kept in the office and released to the prisoners on a monthly basis, one between every two or four men, following which there was always 'an intensive campaign of swapping', with each item allocated an agreed number of points. Milk powder was valued most highly, with 100 points; half a pound of cheese was worth fifty points, six ounces of coffee twenty points, and so on.[19] Some POWs gorged themselves until they vomited; others hoarded their precious goodies, eking them out for weeks.

The ICRC performed a fantastic service during the Second World War, often in the most difficult circumstances. The parcels it distributed to POWs throughout the world invariably lifted spirits and saved countless lives (although there were some camps at which not a single parcel was passed on to the prisoners; if any arrived, the Japanese guards kept them for themselves). At Keijo, the men received not only food and toiletries but clothing, medicines, books, letters, even sports equipment and a gramophone, some from the YMCA but most of it from the Red Cross. Eager to counter the burgeoning rumours in Britain, Australia and the United States about their treatment of prisoners, the *Kempeitai* circulated photographs of the moment when the parcels were opened.

Keijo was inspected twice more by the ICRC, on 15 November 1943 and 29 November 1944. On both occasions, senior Allied officers were allowed to submit a list of questions to the representative, but only after they had been vetted. Each visit was also preceded by a smokescreen of camouflage activity. 'The Japanese put on a special show for him [the representative]', recalled Lt Fuller: 'They gave the POWs a special lunch; allowed them light work that day; the canteen was well stocked for the occasion, but when the Red Cross representative left it was immediately

Opening a Red Cross parcel, Kempeitai photograph in *NIB*

removed'; the whole business was 'a complete farce'. The normally tight-lipped editors of *Nor Iron Bars* agreed: 'There's no end to these window-dressings', they noted in November 1944.[20] There were also suspicions that some of the contents of the parcels were not being passed on, suspicions which were confirmed when one of the sentries was spotted throwing away an empty bully beef tin. Although Col. Elrington complained, nothing was done.

Yet, welcome as the ICRC parcels were, they could never provide more than temporary, marginal relief, and from the summer of 1943, as rations were cut, sickness increased. A year later, at least one officer was being hospitalized every week. Their complaints varied – filariasis, malaria, renal colic, tonsillitis, pleurisy, dysentery – but fundamentally they were weak with malnourishment. When a severe bout of dysentery put John Lever in hospital, the Japanese medical orderly asked him what he thought might help. 'I haven't had an egg for two years,' he replied, but eggs were not available. Instead, he was given some extra bully beef and six ounces of cheese, and within a month had recovered some weight.[21]

Like food, drugs and dressings were also in short supply, but when the prisoners asked to be given more, they were told they must endure, since none was available (which was not true). Thanks largely to the skill of Maj. (Dr) Tom O'Donnell, most of the patients recovered, and Dr Uchida was conscientious in arranging for them to be given inoculations against diphtheria, typhoid and dysentery. He also regularly distributed the Vitamin C tablets which arrived in Red Cross parcels. Even so, from the time the Loyals disembarked at Busan until the day of liberation three years later, twenty-four members of the battalion died in Korea. Although none of these deaths was directly attributable to starvation, almost all resulted from malnourishment or neglect of one kind or another.[22] Yet, although Dr Uchida was far from perfect, and certainly not popular with the officers, whom he refused to treat for two months in 1943 after a perceived slight, he was a lot better than the medical orderly at Jinsen, Dr Mizuguchi – of whom more later.

One factor contributing to the prisoners' ill health was the weather. In summer, the thermometer hovered around the ninety-Fahrenheit mark and was sometimes closer to a hundred. With

> now unwavering, he & Nightingale are now the only regular patients in the hospital. There seems to be no hope for Nightingale.
> My weight at the end of June was 67.3 Kilos. We had our second jab for anti-dysentry. We should be fairly immune from things now with 3 anti-dyptheria jabs 2 T.A.B. 2 anti dysentry & vaccination.
>
> July At the end of July my weight was 67.5 Kilos. Had some stomach trouble at the beginning of the month but it got better.
> Tomatoes are growing on our plants on the private plot. We have had something like 2000 lbs. of tomatoes from the communal lot & expect in all about 4000 lbs. Tomatoes & odd things from the Red Cross parcels are very useful augmentations to the eternal infernal rice & stew. I can't understand why, in a country like this, with this climate, the natives live so poorly and grow such a lot of rubbishy stuff. Rice is unappetizing stuff and doesn't get the gastric juices flowing. It doesn't make your mouth water and eating is just a necessity instead of something to look forward to with pleasurable anticipation. The natives themselves suffer from vitamin deficiency which has to be made up for with jabs or Wakamoto tablets & so forth. Our private plot tomatoes should be ready to eat in 2 weeks or so; we also have corn, pumpkins, onions, cabbage & cucumber.
> Went to Rusan Stn. twice with working parties, got some cigarettes the second visit. The troops seem to manage to do more harm than good. I understand a contractor pays 2 ¥ per day per man, each man gets 10 cents & the camp 90 s.

A page from John Lever's diary, June–July 1943

no fans available, 'we just lay on our mats in a lather', fighting the lice and fleas, although at least they had mosquito nets. But it was winter that was the real trial. For Henling Wade, who had lived through Chinese winters, 'the coldest days I ever experienced were in Korea'.[23] Their bitterest night at Keijo was 27 January 1945, when there were forty degrees of frost (minus twenty-one Celsius), but every winter saw heavy snowfalls and there were weeks on end when even the temperature in the mess-rooms never rose above freezing. Yet not until late November or early December were the stoves brought into the squad-rooms, and by mid-March they had been removed again. The POWs would spend the winter evenings huddled around them, swathed in blankets on top of their ex-Japanese army greatcoats. Worst of all was waking up in the night and realizing that you had to go to the *benjo*, an outhouse several metres from the main building – for, as one poetaster's Dog Latin put it, '*Mucke et Deplorum est depissere in lite*' (a charitable translation of which would be 'It is dirty and shameful to piss in your bed').[24] When dysentery struck, as it so often did, the outcome was doubly embarrassing. Henling Wade recalled that 'all night long men ran down the stairs of our warehouse half-clad, hoping to reach the *benjo* in time, but often failing'.[25] The agony of the moment is captured in an aria to the tune of Gilbert and Sullivan's 'Tit-Willow', from an operetta based on the *Mikado* performed in the camp early in 1943:

> On a bed in the officers' mess a man lay
> Sighing Benjo, O Benjo, O Benjo.
> And I said to him tell me now why do you say
> O Benjo, O Benjo, O Benjo?
> Did the gruel for breakfast upset your inside,
> Or the *leggi*[26] that you couldn't eat though you tried?
> With a shake of his head and a groan he replied,
> O Benjo, O Benjo, O Benjo.
>
> Then moaning he rose and rushed with a cry
> To the Benjo, the Benjo, the Benjo.
> And I'm sure as can be that I understand why
> He ran to the Benjo, the Benjo, the Benjo.
> It isn't the gruel or *leggis*, but it's
> Those curséd stewed turnips that gave him the squits
> And made him rush off to those bottomless pits
> Of the Benjo, the Benjo, the Benjo.[27]

Chamber pots would have saved the prisoners a lot of discomfort (*NIB*)

PRISONER STORIES

Bombardier Butler

Cornelius Dirk Punt, a Dutch POW on the Burma–Thailand railway,[28] told the following story of a group of 'sturdy and aggressive' Australians whom he accompanied one day in 1943 on a working-party in the Burmese jungle:

> Two Japs, bayonets fixed, escorted these fifty-odd walking bags of bones under the hot sun to a railway job. Hunger was written on every face; hunger was shining in every eye. Wearily the prisoners walked along, without noticing in the distance a native figure approaching along the narrow path. It was a young Burmese woman, dressed in a colourful lungyi – the sarong – which by the more primitive in these parts is worn in a fashion similar to the style in Bali. The neckline of this fastidious native girl from lower Burma started at the hips. With springtime in her steps the young woman rapidly came nearer, balancing on her head a large woven tray with golden ripe bananas. Gradually one might have detected a reaction in the eyes of the marching men. First a few, then all the prisoners noticed that the jungle track was not deserted. When the girl was a few feet away, every man had his eyes on what attracted him most. One digger, too eager to control a comment, summed up the feelings of every man when he exclaimed, 'Look at those bloody bananas!'

Punt's story chimes with a belief restated often enough to have become axiomatic: that prisoners of the Japanese were so debilitated by hunger that they almost completely lost their appetite for sex. And so it may well have been on the Death Railway, or indeed at many other camps: 'Starving men don't have sex urges,' declared Henling Wade, 'all we craved was food.'[29] Where life was less dire, however, things were a little different, at least in the fecund imaginations of thousands of young men deprived of female company for years on end. At Keijo, one of the few benefits of going out on a

Dreaming POW (*NIB*)

work-party was that it afforded opportunities to see women: 'Girls in "miso" shop not visible today but a nice bit of frippet near the police station,' commented one officer on his return to camp.[30] Men dreamed of women, they sketched or painted sinuous young women, and they wrote wistful poems to chimerical lovers:

> Lady, if I say I loved you like I never loved before,
> If (to vary the above) you stir me daily more and more,
> With a deeper, warmer passion that I've known in my career,
> 'Tis because the present fashion of my life is so austere.
>
> Lady, I shall never meet you, I can never cause you shame,
> By the mode in which I greet you, for I do not know your name.
> You're compound of Belle and Nancy, Madeleine and Guinevere,
> Distillation of my fancy – and my life is so austere.[31]

But there was, of course, an alternative. A question Wade was constantly asked after the war was whether there had been any homosexuality between prisoners. He replied that he had heard in Omori (Japan) that 'one or two hungry young men had offered themselves', but there were no takers, and he came away 'entirely convinced that there had been no homosexuality in the camps I'd been in'.[32] Australian POWs were either less guarded or more observant: at Changi, said one AIF private, 'homosexuals were about, and what's more, did a trade – only to be expected, I suppose'. Another remembered 'a few poofters' at a camp in New Guinea, but the attitude towards them was one of 'deep disapproval'. At Omuta, a large coal-mining camp on Kyushu, about twenty-five homosexual couples sought counselling from American and Dutch doctors on how to cope with the 'almost universal homophobia' of the POWs. Even in Thailand, said one POW, 'homosexuality was evident … doctors said the rice diet had much to do with it' – not an explanation to command universal acceptance.[33]

One unsettling source of ambivalence were the concerts put on at even the grimmest camps, for those who played female parts were usually young and good-looking, and, as one prisoner put it, 'to be able to feast the eyes on something that looked like a woman was a powerful thing. And complicated.' According to Wade, the best female impersonators were 'frankly adored – the only people about whom there was any glamour'. Even the Japanese guards offered them flowers or chocolates.[34] And few if any were better than Bombardier Arthur Butler of 122 Field Regiment, Royal Artillery, Keijo Camp's most celebrated inmate.

Long before he arrived at Keijo, Butler was well known on the Far East colonial concert circuit, where he adopted the stage name Gloria d'Earie. Before the war, his 'delightful tenor voice' could be heard on Radio Singapore every Sunday; he was in constant demand for birthday parties and had even performed for the Sultan of Johore. A fellow soldier remembered that Butler had once spent an afternoon and evening in the bar at Raffles Hotel dressed as Gloria without being outed. According to Wade, he was 'slim and gracious, with small features and ardent brown eyes.' Another soldier described his female *alter ego* as 'exquisite

– makes all "her" own dresses and wears them beautifully. Every look and gesture completely feminine.'[35] Butler spent the full three years at Keijo, where the chief impresario of camp concerts, Capt. Jack McNaughton of the Loyals, who had been a West End actor before the war, always chose him as his leading 'lady'. Fortunately a bout of diphtheria on the *Fukai Maru* had dimmed none of Butler's talents and his appearances were invariably the star turn. According to Wade, the gunners in his platoon routinely addressed him, without reproof, as 'darling' (although perhaps he meant to write 'dearie').[36]

Sex was indeed a complicated thing in a POW camp.

Bombardier Butler as Gloria d'Earie, Keijo concert hall, Christmas 1943, Kempeitai photo

FOUR

Insincerity

For many of the 460 POWs originally sent there, Keijo was, like Changi, a transit camp. Apart from the Loyals, who made up the majority, the two main cohorts were from the Yorkshire-based 122 Regiment, Field Artillery, and the Australian Imperial Force (AIF), scores of whom were transferred when needed to camps at Jinsen, Mukden in Manchuria, or, when it opened in September 1943, Konan. There were also new arrivals and returnees. Numbers at Keijo thus fluctuated greatly. By June 1944 there were only 159 prisoners left, and by Christmas just seventy-nine, of whom forty-five were officers, but by August 1945 the total was up to 166. The one constant in Keijo's POW population was the Loyals' officer cadre, most of whom spent the full three years there. An exception was Henling Wade, one of the original three editors of *Nor Iron Bars*, who was told in November 1943 that he would be transferred in two days' time to a camp on the Japanese mainland. He was 'aghast' at the news: 'I didn't want to go. Life was bearable in [Keijo] … I was sorry to be leaving this camp.' He feared something much worse, and he was right. He later reckoned that during the last twenty-one months of the war, first at Omori camp and then at Naoetsu, he was slapped, punched or kicked about 350 times, roughly once every two days.[1] As a result, he came to look back on his time at Keijo, like the POWs who returned from Burma or Thailand to Changi, with a certain nostalgia. Yet these were differences of degree, not of kind, for physical punishment was far from uncommon at Keijo, especially during the later stages of the war, after Wade left. What is arguably most revealing about his comments is how the prisoners had come to define 'bearable'.

Scarcely had they arrived when the POWs were given a foretaste of what 'medical care' meant at Keijo. One of the many Loyals who had left the *Fukai Maru* suffering from severe dysentery was Pte Metcalf, who had to be carried to the camp. While Noguchi first addressed and then detained them in the exercise yard, Metcalf 'was left on the open square on a stretcher in the terrific heat of the sun for about two hours. He was writhing in pain and delirious.' Although his condition had been reported on arrival to the camp doctor Uchida, it was not until detention was over that he was taken to the hospital, where he died three weeks later.[2] When Uchida was later tried for war crimes, numerous witnesses testified to his callous treatment of sick men. Although Red Cross and other medicines were available, they were often denied to the POWs and used instead to treat the Japanese and Korean guards. When the YMCA sent drugs and dressings, Uchida simply locked them away. Men who were manifestly too sick were nevertheless made to work, even in temperatures of minus ten or fifteen Celsius. There were only ten camp beds in the on-site infirmary, and severely ill men were often kept waiting for weeks before being transferred to the nearby military hospital. Dental care was almost non-existent – according to one report, a dentist appeared only once in eighteen months.[3] When Col. Elrington (acting on the advice of Dr O'Donnell, who had a 'very low' opinion of Uchida's medical competence) refused to accept an injection which Uchida wanted to give him, Uchida became so angry that he refused to treat any officers for two months. In the opinion of several POWs, he was indirectly responsible for the deaths of several men not only at Keijo but also at the Jinsen and Konan branch camps, where he failed to exercise adequate medical supervision. The latter charges were not upheld by the IMT, but for his neglect of the sick at Keijo he was sentenced in 1947 to twelve years' imprisonment with hard labour. Tatsumi Ushihara, a medical orderly at Keijo who had graduated from the University of California and doubled as camp interpreter, was also said to have taken 'great delight in mistreating the sick, making free use of his fists to inflict blows to their faces'. He was probably lucky to get away with a sentence of ten years with hard labour, which the judge advocate at his trial described as 'hardly adequate for the crimes of which he was convicted'.[4]

The war crimes trials held under the auspices of the International Military Tribunal at Tokyo and Yokohama have been labelled as 'Victors' Justice', and in a sense they obviously were, but the transcripts of their proceedings suggest that they were conducted with considerable care. Depositions were taken from numerous witnesses, the defendants were permitted to put their case and on the majority of charges they were found not guilty. Verdicts were subsequently reviewed, petitions for clemency were considered, and many of the longer sentences were reduced.[5] In many instances, however, the evidence was overwhelming.

This was certainly the case with the thirty-seven-year-old former farmer and policeman Lt Takeo Terada, who according to Lever was 'our most heartily detested Japanese officer'.[6] Terada was hard to avoid. As the 'intendant and senior guard', he lived with his wife and six children in the compound's married quarters, which adjoined the office, giving him ample opportunities to misappropriate the contents of the Red Cross parcels stored there. Several POWs later testified that when they cleared out his rubbish bins they often found empty or half empty ICRC tins or packets of bully beef, milk, chocolate, cheese and cigarettes.[7] Yet it was for his beatings that Terada was chiefly feared. He used his fists, his feet, the butt of his rifle, a sheathed sword, or anything that else that came to hand, such as sticks or heavy rolls of paper. Many of these 'bashings' were administered in the guardroom. An Australian POW, Pte Clarke, had written a letter to his wife in February 1943 stating that without Red Cross parcels the POWs could not have survived. Brought before Terada and Ushihara (who often seem to have operated together), he was told by the latter that this was insulting. Ushihara then 'struck him across the face with his clenched fist', following which

> Ushihara spoke to Terada and the latter punched him around the head and body and kicked him in the shins. Terada picked up a sword stick made of cane and struck him with all his force on his head and body. The bashing continued for about two

hours in the evening. His body and face were black and blue from the beating. His left eye was blackened and he had lumps on his head like eggs. A tooth was broken off his lower denture and his cheek was cut inside.

Clarke was then taken to the isolation cell, where he was kept in solitary confinement for ten days 'in conditions of extreme cold without adequate bedding or food'.[8]

According to some of the men, 'it was a common occurrence for Terada to brutally assault POWs for no apparent reason'. He also used to deliver 'pep talks' haranguing the Korean guards to be stricter with the working parties, following which 'we were sure to be bashed'.[9] John Lever found himself physically disgusted by such incidents, but although 'the satisfaction of flattening one of the creatures' would have been enormously appealing, self-control was essential, as Pte Lomasney, of the Loyals, discovered to his cost.[10] Early in 1943 he found an empty tin of Red Cross bully beef which he knew that one of the guards must have eaten, which he reported to the office. After this 'he was closely watched and beaten for no apparent reason'. Then on 6 March he was hit by a Korean overseer who accused him of being lazy. Lomasney 'pushed the overseer away', and when one of the sentries joined in, he also 'pushed the sentry away'. He was promptly taken to the guardroom, where Terada 'hit him and kicked him several times', then continued to beat him with a sheathed samurai sword.

But much worse was to come. Because he was deemed to have retaliated, Lomasney was sentenced to three years in Seidaimon civilian jail in Keijo. Seidaimon was a fearsome place. According to the chief jailer, the POWs confined there 'did not have enough clothing, heat, medicine, food – enough of anything'.[11] When Lomasney was first taken there he was interrogated by the *Kempeitai*; when he refused to sign a confession implicating other POWs, he was punched so hard that he was knocked off his chair and then 'crowned on the head with the chair'.[12] Two British lieutenants, Roger Pigott and Joe Moore, both in their early twenties, died after being sent to Seidaimon. Moore and another POW, Sgt Bosworth, had tried to escape to Russia but were quickly recaptured. Seven others, including Pigott, were accused of helping them, or at least knowing their plans. After interrogation by the *Kempeitai*, they were all sent to Seidaimon: Moore and Bosworth were given eight and six years respectively, their accomplices two or three. Moore survived for less than a year, dying in April 1944. Pigott contracted pleurisy but lingered until the end of the war, when he was taken back to the camp, where he died on 29 August 1945 of tubercular meningitis.

Col. Elrington complained vigorously to Noguchi about Pte Lomasney's treatment, as he did about many matters, one of which was the striking of officers. Noguchi had given him assurances, and apparently instructed his subordinates, that officers should not be hit, but Terada took little notice of this. Both *Nor Iron Bars* and the 1947 trial transcript record dozens of cases of officers being slapped. Not untypical was an incident which occurred in the early summer of 1944. About a dozen officers had gone to work in the officers' garden:

> The work was entirely voluntary. During the morning break they were all sitting in a small hut which had one small window. Terada came to the hut and entered the door from behind. He struck Lt Fuller a heavy blow on the face with his open hand; he went along the row and struck the others in the same manner. A few minutes later an interpreter arrived and told them they had been hit because they did not stand up and salute Terada.

At his trial, Terada admitting hitting the officers, saying that they had lied to him by claiming that they had not saluted him because they had not seen him.[13] Yet although the presumption that officers should not be hit was often breached, it does seem to have been accepted in principle, at least by Col. Noguchi. Shortly before he left Keijo, Henling Wade was slapped hard on each cheek by a Japanese officer for failing to salute him. When Elrington complained, the officer in question tried to hush it up, and a 'half-hearted apology' was later offered. Another guard who slapped an officer tried to excuse himself by saying that he had just been engaging in 'a bit of shadow-boxing'. Terada was also told off by Noguchi more than once for slapping officers; on one occasion, when he admitted hitting a major, Noguchi became 'very angry' with him. However, the POWs believed that there

Sentry and small boy salute the night-soil cart, a lampoon on the Japanese insistence on being saluted (*NIB*)

were many things that Terada kept from his commandant. At his trial in 1947, he was described by the judge advocate as a 'cruel and contemptible' man who 'exulted in his arrogant power' and inflicted 'untold suffering' on his prisoners. He was sentenced to thirty-seven years with hard labour, reduced on review to thirty-three.[14]

Lt Terada was one of a type commonly found in Japanese POW camps. Even if the commander was a reasonable man (and many were not), there always seems to have been a second or third or fourth in command, often of quite lowly rank, who enjoyed beating or humiliating or inflicting egregious forms of torture on the prisoners: men such as the 'unmitigated brutal bastard' Lt Abe, who simply ignored the scruples of his weak and aging commander at Sonkurai camp on the Burma–Thailand railway; or Sgt Mori, to whom his 'lazy' commander at Haruku, Lt Kurashima, more or less abdicated responsibility for running the camp; or Cpl Matsuhiro Watanabe at Omori, who, according to Henling Wade, seemed through sheer force of personality to be able to countermand orders from his seniors and inflict any kind of punishment that he wanted on the prisoners. Wade speculated that he might secretly have been a member of the *Kempeitai* (who certainly had their 'spies' in some camps) or of the feared Black Dragon Society, responsible for several political assassinations in Japan during the 1930s. After the war, Sgt Mori and Lt Abe were both condemned to death by hanging, although Abe's sentence was commuted to fifteen years' imprisonment. When a former POW at Sonkurai met him in Tokyo in 1995, he apparently expressed 'considerable remorse' for his behaviour. As for Cpl Watanabe, he managed to evade both the American and the Japanese police and in 1989 was reported to be still alive and well and living in Tokyo.[15]

There were all sorts of reasons why a POW might be given a slap or a kick at Keijo: for smoking at prohibited times or too far away from an ashtray, failing to salute or bow to a sentry, whistling at work, not working fast enough, numbering incorrectly or stepping out of line or being late at roll-call, keeping a disorderly barrack-room, grumbling about the food, and numerous other petty infractions. An Australian POW, Pte Vynall, who was found sketching in the exercise yard, was dealt a heavy blow behind the ear with a rifle butt and made to stand in the guardhouse for three days, where he was not permitted to lie, crouch or lean against the wall. When he dozed off while standing up on the third day, he was roused with a kick in the stomach which left him bruised for a month.[16] There was nothing gentle about the Japanese slap: one or two of the sentries used to stand on a bed or jump in the air while slapping to achieve additional impetus.[17] Men might have lifelong injuries after beatings, such as damaged eardrums or broken noses. After Pte Leigh was beaten and kicked for two hours by three sentries in June 1943, he lost two teeth, his lips were bleeding, and his nose was still visibly misshapen three years later. Cpl Fredericks, an Australian, was repeatedly kicked and had three ribs broken.[18]

Running Terada a close second at Keijo was Masataro Takuma, a quick-tempered twenty-two-year-old sergeant with a 'vicious nature' who regularly hit officers and men alike and was later sentenced to thirty-one years with hard labour, reduced on review to twenty-five. The deed for which he became notorious occurred during a working-party in February 1944 when he struck a British POW, Pte Mackenzie, three or four times on each side of the face with an improvised soup ladle made from 'a piece of wood with an empty meat can nailed at the end, with the pointed ends of nails protruding'. Mackenzie's 'ear was split and deep grooves were left in his face'. When the British officer accompanying the party

'Chaser' sentry harassing a POW on a working-party (*IDS*)

objected, Takuma ordered the six Korean sentries with him to beat the other thirty or so men in the squad, which they did with their fists. Two men fainted from the blows, but were kicked while on the ground, then hauled to their feet and struck again. After this Takuma was known throughout the camp as 'Scoops'.[19] Coining nicknames for the guards was one way of trying to mitigate the nastiness of life in the camp. Various Japanese guards were known as 'the Pig', 'Tom Thumb', 'Cagney', 'the Kicker', 'Peaches and Cream', 'Squint Face' and 'Suki', while three of the less pleasant Korean sentries were known as 'Smoko', 'Paddy' and 'Smiler'.[20] Poems or articles in *Nor Iron Bars* also helped to let off steam. The customary prelude to a beating was for a prisoner to be told, 'You have not been sincere' – the guards' way of informing him that he had broken his promise to obey the camp rules. A poem in the Christmas 1943 issue of *NIB* took up this theme:

So you were hit by a Japanese twit!
Well, you don't observe the rules,
You think they are made for fools?
That's not sincere.
Your outlook is black, on duty you slack,
We don't like contempt in your look.
That's why they've brought you to book.
You're not sincere.
Out working you're bad, on roll-call a cad,
And yet you would have the cheek
To put your case to the Beak.
You can't be sincere.
It's quite out of place, you'll make us lose face,
Such a thing cannot be,
You'll insult Mr. T.[21]
That's most insincere.

Prisoners being searched on a working-party (*SPK*)

Pilfering food was definitely insincere. Working-parties were sent out to several sites around Keijo, one of which was the warehouse at the railway station. Here the POWs loaded or unloaded sacks of provisions and could not resist the temptation to fill socks or pockets with 'liberated' supplies. Two privates caught stealing sugar in January 1944 were first slapped by a sentry, then told to slap each other while the guards watched. A month later, when pilfering was discovered at the farm where a group of around thirty prisoners was working, they were all lined up and slapped in turn.

Apart from slapping and kicking, the commonest form of punishment at Keijo was to be placed in solitary confinement in one of the unheated and barely furnished cells in the guardroom. Two metres by three, these were windowless and lacked ventilation apart from a series of spaced planks in the half-height door. For the first night or two, the prisoner would be allowed all his bedding and normal rations, after which he would be reduced to just two blankets and nothing to eat but rice and salt. After a few days the sentries would take him out to wash, then return him to the cell. The two privates who had stolen sugar from the warehouse in January 1944 were given ten and seven days in the cells. Prisoners caught stealing an apple or smoking at the wrong time were sentenced to eight days, while an Australian private who was caught writing a Christmas card with an insulting reference to Prime Minister Tojo was given twenty-one days. This was in August, when the heat and humidity were almost as unbearable as the January cold.[22]

Corporal punishment of this kind was an extension of Japanese Imperial Army discipline (a point that was later employed as a legal defence at the trials of some guards accused of war crimes).[23] Senior officers slapped junior officers, who slapped their troops, who slapped anyone over whom they could pull rank. At Keijo, this meant the despised Korean guards. In October 1944, when most of the Korean sentries retired after serving their time, Scoops decided to show their replacements how to go about their business by engaging in a round of slapping. Despite their reputation for cruelty, the Koreans were also victims, as indeed were many of the Japanese themselves. In the opinion of Col. Elrington – and of many others both then and since – the fault lay with the system rather than the individual.[24] Threatened with beatings themselves if they allowed the POWs to slack, it is hardly surprising that the sentries complied. However, there is no evidence that Keijo witnessed the grimly inventive repertoire of punishments which the worst Japanese camp commanders honed almost to an art form, such as repeatedly jumping from a table on to a spread-eagled man, confinement for days in crates so small that it was impossible to stand or lie down, or the notorious 'rice and water' procedure.[25] Even John Lever conceded that 'there are one or two of the Japs [at Keijo] you could mistake for gentlemen by closing your eyes to a few things'.[26]

That there was less brutality at Keijo than at most other Japanese camps was due in large part to Col. Noguchi. Although he was sentenced to twenty-two years with hard labour at the Yokohama War Trials, this was primarily on the principle of command responsibility, not just at Keijo but also at Jinsen and Konan. At Konan especially, where the POWs stoked the furnaces in a carbide factory, conditions were generally thought to be considerably worse than at Keijo, but it was difficult for Noguchi to visit his two branch camps more than once or twice a month and much went on behind his back. One of the charges on which he was found guilty was failing to control Dr Mizuguchi at Jinsen, yet prisoners there said that they looked forward to Noguchi's visits because they would be given better rations and no one would be beaten in his presence; at Konan, the temperature in the furnaces would be turned down for the day. Even at Keijo, the POWs noticed that the guards rarely struck them while Noguchi was watching and that he sometimes got angry with his subordinates for being unnecessarily harsh – indeed, he eventually had Scoops removed from the camp. In October 1944, when he heard that one of his underlings had told the prisoners to hand their diaries in to the office, he countermanded the order, declaring that 'diaries were for writing one's own private thoughts and we could not be censured for writing anything we thought'.[27] Col. Elrington thought that a lot went on which Noguchi did not know about, although Dr O'Donnell was not so sure, noting that severe beatings sometimes took place in his presence and that it was on his orders that Red Cross medicines were held back.[28]

Yet according to Henling Wade, by comparison with other camp commanders he encountered Noguchi was 'an honourable man', 'a decent, humane individual' who did not abuse his power at Keijo, as a result of which the camp was run in a 'correct, decent and disciplined fashion'. Col. Elrington described him as 'a mild middle-aged man anxious for a quiet life'.[29] For the judges at his trial, this was clearly not good enough: a man entrusted with the lives of over 1,000 prisoners should have made greater efforts to ensure their safety. Yet one notable fact distinguished Noguchi from the worst type of Japanese camp commander: despite his warnings about escape attempts, which were often punishable by beheading, there were no executions at any of his camps. 'His bark was worse than his bite', and although he may well have fulfilled his responsibilities indifferently, his sentence of twenty-two years appears harsh for a man against whom very little evidence of deliberate brutality was produced and whose trial, it has been claimed, 'took several shortcuts'.[30] The regime which he oversaw at Keijo was not marked by routine brutality, which was restricted to a relatively small number of unpleasant individuals. In the event, none of them served more than ten years in prison, for following the restoration of Japan's sovereignty in 1952 and its admission to the United Nations in 1956, the clamour for its war criminals to be pardoned grew ever stronger, and by 1958 they had all been unconditionally released.[31]

PRISONER STORIES

Dr Mizuguchi

Yasutoshi Mizuguchi was an accomplished musician and an athlete noted for his sportsmanship and sense of fair play. He had a medical degree from the Imperial University at Keijo. After graduating, his 'Christian-like benevolence' had induced him to risk his life by serving in a 5,000-strong leper colony where he was said to have effected a number of cures. To the prisoners in his care, however, he was 'a sadist', and for his 'diabolical conduct' as senior medical officer at Jinsen he earned the dubious distinction of being the only official at the three POW camps in Korea to be sentenced to death.[32]

Dr Mizuguchi arrived at Jinsen in May 1944, aged thirty and divorced. The most serious charges against him were that, by either abusing or failing to provide medicines or adequate treatment for two American prisoners, Lt William King and Capt. George Brundrett, he had 'contributed to and accelerated' their death. After King's death on 14 May 1945, he had also threatened to beat the senior American officer at Jinsen, Col. Curtis Beecher (himself a sick man), unless he agreed to sign a false death certificate saying that King had died of heart failure. Beecher had already been punched and kicked by Mizuguchi on several occasions and knew that he did not hesitate to strike officers, however senior. Of the twelve charges of abuse against Mizuguchi in which individual POWs were named, eight concerned officers (including three colonels). He was also said to have forced numerous prisoners to work when unfit to do so.

The American POWs at Jinsen had been transferred from the Philippines and only arrived in April 1945. More than half of them were suffering from dysentery and/or beriberi, and a few were very sick indeed. On the whole they found the conditions at Jinsen better than in the Philippines, but not the medical care. Mizuguchi's default diagnosis for POWs who attended his

> This is to certify that 2nd Lieutenant KING WILLIAM MILLAGE, American prisoner of war, who had been unfit due to the physical deficiencies before he was taken into this camp, The Chosen Prisoner of War Camp No.1 Branch Camp, has been suffering from enteritis since the beginning of May, and taking a favourable turn with a proper medical treatment, suddenly died of HEART FAILURE at 7.30 A.M. on the 14th, May, 20th of Showa.
>
> Curtis J. Beecher
> Lt. Col. U.S.M.C.

Death certificate of William King signed by Col. Beecher

dispensary seems to have been that they were trying to shirk. A British doctor at Jinsen, Capt. Gibbs, stated that only if a man was unable to walk would Mizuguchi excuse him from work. Although Red Cross medicines were received, they were rarely distributed, and requests for dressings were constantly denied; even to ask for them was to risk a beating. When Maj. Holohan, the senior British officer at Jinsen, put in a request to speak with the camp commander, Col. Okazaki, Mizuguchi intercepted it. The next day, Holohan 'was sent for by Mizuguchi and asked if he still wished to see Okazaki. When he replied that he did, Mizuguchi beat him brutally.' Although Lt Isobe, 'a friendly Japanese officer', apologised to Holohan, Mizuguchi later beat him again. The doctor was 'a powerfully built man', and several POWs at Jinsen testified that he enjoyed testing his capacity to inflict pain. Men were left with teeth driven through their lips, faces or ankles so grossly swollen that for days they could not eat or stand, deafness from broken eardrums or blood poisoning from untreated cuts, but they dared not complain to Col. Okazaki because Mizuguchi would invariably hear of it and beat them again. These beatings were recorded in the camp diary as 'disciplinary warnings'.

Yet it was primarily because he was found guilty of direct responsibility for the deaths of Lt King and Capt. Brundrett that Mizuguchi was condemned to hang. Col. Jack Schwartz, the senior American doctor at Jinsen, described Brundrett's last weeks as follows:

> He had to move his bowels six or eight times a day. He had a severe case of oedema on his ankles and feet; his feet were swollen to twice the normal size. He could not wear his shoes and had to walk barefooted ... About 1 June 1945 he began to show a swelling and pitting oedema of the lower extremities up to the waist ... [Schwartz] asked Sasaki, the Japanese medical orderly, for plasma. Sasaki took it from the shelf to give it to him, but before he administered it, Mizuguchi refused to allow the plasma to be given. [Schwartz] made four or five more requests for the plasma, but was refused. Two or three days before Brundrett's death, when he was in an unconscious condition, the plasma was given, but the case was so hopeless that [Schwartz] did not use it.[33]

Schwartz also requested amebicides, but these too were refused. When he asked Okazaki to move Brundrett to hospital, Mizuguchi severely chastised him for 'going over his head'. Capt. Brundrett died on 4 July 1945. According to Schwartz, 'his death was attributable to the neglect and maltreatment of Mizuguchi, who knew his condition'. The tribunal agreed.

Three weeks before Japan's surrender, Mizuguchi absconded from Jinsen, but early in October 1945 he was apprehended and charged. Two years later, after sentence was pronounced, several petitions for clemency were submitted by friends, parents, brothers and sisters, but upon review by Col. A. R. Browne, the Army Judge Advocate, they were not considered sufficient to outweigh the tribunal's view that he 'should be removed from the society of decent men'. Although Mizuguchi's sister submitted a petition begging that his life be spared, she added, 'We Japanese have deep respect for and bear no resentment against the fair trials according to justice and humanity.' This was 'gratifying', commented Col. Browne, but it did not save her brother.

FIVE

Rank

ONE OF THE REASONS FOR COL. NOGUCHI's relatively benign regime at Keijo was because he was following orders. Japanese army command had not originally planned to send any POWs to Korea. They changed their minds because they wanted to 'demonstrate Japan's imperial might to its Korean colonial subjects' and 'stamp out the respect and admiration of Koreans for Britain and America'.[1] This is why the proportion of officers to men at Keijo was so much higher than in most of its camps: because high-ranking prisoners would impress the Koreans more than enlisted soldiers. From the moment it opened, then, Keijo was planned as a 'show camp', a propaganda vehicle to present to the world the face that Japan wanted to be seen. That is why it was one of only a small minority of camps where Red Cross inspections were permitted and parcels distributed on a regular basis. Of the 200 or so POW camps that Japan operated between 1942 and 1945, only about half a dozen were show camps. Changi was one, Zentsuji on Shikoku island (Japan) was another, and at least one ICRC visit was permitted at Woosung, near Shanghai.[2] That is also why the *Kempeitai* periodically visited the camp to take photographs or make newsreels, some of which were shown not just in Japan but in cinemas around the world.

By late 1943, however, the Japanese seem to have given up trying to convince a disbelieving world that they treated their POWs humanely, and Keijo's show status was abandoned.[3] At this point things might have got a lot worse, but the POWs at Keijo were also lucky in another respect – their Senior Officer. If Col. Noguchi was an honourable man, said Henling Wade, 'Col Elrington was equally honourable, presenting our case to the Japanese in a calm,

A page of regimental badges with (below) signatures of officers at Keijo.
The Loyals in the middle (*NIB*)

quiet voice, which Noguchi respected'.[4] Mordaunt 'Bill' Elrington, DSO, MC (and later OBE), was a tall, trim, softly-spoken man of unmistakable military bearing, the sort that the Japanese often enjoyed cutting down to size, but he and Noguchi soon established a good working relationship: when Elrington had matters to discuss – which usually meant to request – Noguchi would invite him to the office and they would share a cup of tea. It helped that they had met before, at the outbreak of the Sino-Japanese war in August 1937, when the Loyals were mobilised to patrol the Shanghai Bund and protect the International Settlement.[5]

Elrington also enjoyed the confidence of his fellow officers. 'There are certain individuals of this Mess,' wrote the editors of *Nor Iron Bars* in the Christmas 1942 issue, 'who, during the past few months, have been working unceasingly for the improvement of conditions and for the general benefit of all', and to whom they wished to pay tribute. These were Elrington, Capt. Paque the adjutant, Capt. Sullivan the former garrison adjutant, and Maj. (Dr) O'Donnell.[6] Despite spending several months in hospital with acute bronchitis,[7] Elrington regularly sought interviews with Noguchi or his second-in command, Capt. Goto, to request extra

Message of thanks to senior officers (*NIB*, Christmas 1942)

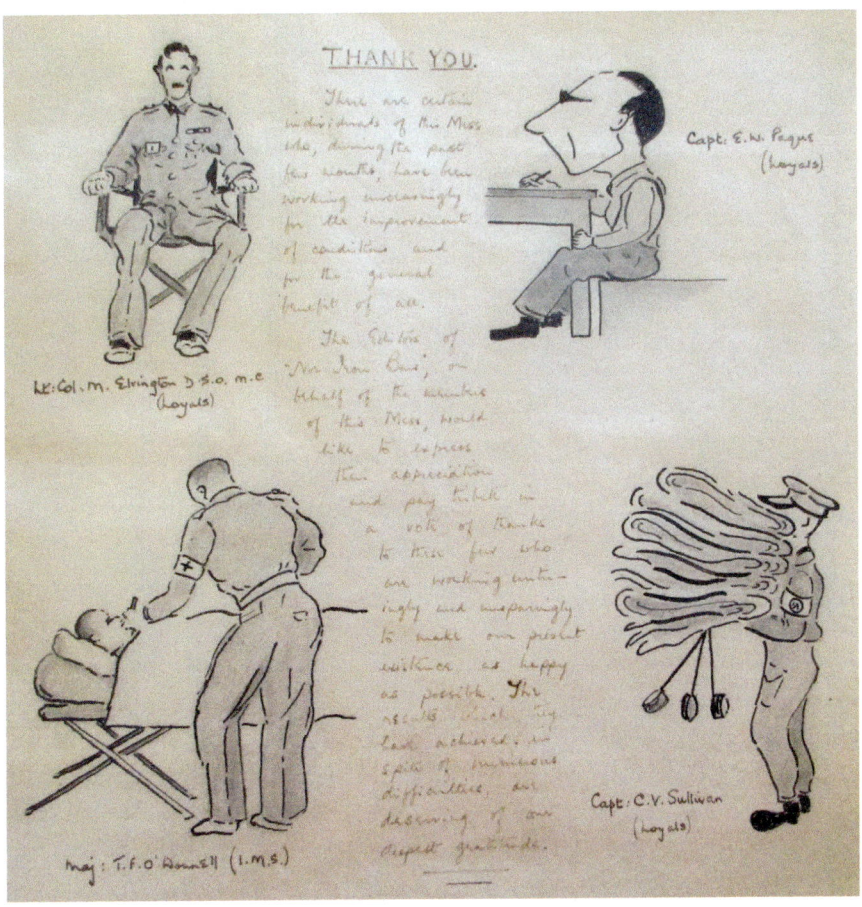

medical supplies, better rations, or the mitigation of punitive measures.⁸ If Noguchi demurred, Elrington pressurised him into coming before the prisoners to explain himself.

Nor was it just the officers who respected Elrington. Sgt Dick Swarbrick of the Loyals thought him 'a fine soldier' and recalled a radio conversation he had overheard during the final stages of the battle for Singapore, when Elrington 'told the officer at the other end of the line that if he withdrew then he, Elrington, would personally come and find him and shoot him'. His determination to fight to the last also earned the respect of his opposite number, for as soon as the ceasefire took effect a Japanese colonel made his way across the battle-scarred ground to where Elrington was standing and witnesses heard the following exchange: 'I wish to congratulate you and your men on your defence. How many men have you?' 'A hundred and twenty-nine.' 'Is that all?' 'Yes.' 'What other troops are there here?' 'No more here. Beyond that hill there are a few.' 'So! You are to be congratulated. You have opposite you a division.'⁹ Elrington's leadership in war, albeit in a lost cause, set him apart from the general run of officers in the Malaya campaign, whom their enlisted men had little hesitation in blaming for the debacle (while the officers in turn blamed the 'brass hats', especially Percival).

Apart from Elrington, the only other POW permitted to enter the camp office was Capt. E. W. 'Jiminy' Paque, battalion adjutant and liaison officer. Like his C.O., Paque was a Loyal through and through. On the morning after Singapore surrendered, he and Elrington jointly sent a message to be read out to all ranks: 'I congratulate you on fighting so well. Through no fault of yours we have been ordered to surrender. Remember the lads who fought and died, and show the same spirit of duty and discipline in defeat. Do nothing to bring discredit on the Loyals as prisoners of war. God bless you.'¹⁰ Yet the two men were very different. Paque stood no nonsense from the guards. Built like a bulldog, with a booming laugh, fearsome black eyebrows and a chin of granite, he had no compunction in telling sentries who were harassing prisoners to 'Clear off!' 'Who the hell do you think you are to give me orders?' he once barked at the interpreter Ushihara. And somehow, he got away with it, for there is no record of him ever being struck.

'Jiminy' Paque, Loyals battalion adjutant (*NIB*)

Between them, in their very different ways, he and Elrington did their best for the men, and not just for the officers.

Sitting a little uncomfortably alongside Elrington's duty of care towards the men was his responsibility for ensuring the observance of his officers' privileges. About a month after arriving at Keijo, he asked Noguchi to allocate the officers accommodation in a separate building (as specified in the Geneva Convention). Noguchi's response was to line the officers up and give them a lecture: 'As regards your warrant officers, NCOs and men, you appear to despise them. You are arrogant and haughty and my advice to you is to study your men and change your views. In the Japanese army we do not despise our men, but all are members of a happy family.'[11] This was not simply a question of believing that privileges should be earned rather than assumed: 'the Japanese mind', wrote Lever, 'if it can condone anything, says "if one man has, all men must have".' This was clearly not a mentality that appealed to some of the British officer class, yet, whatever the 'other ranks' thought of the Japanese army as a 'happy family', there were undoubtedly some among them who would have agreed with Noguchi. Henling Wade, who had begun his career as a 'five-dollar private' before officer training, considered most British officers to be 'stuffy', 'cliquey', 'undemonstrative strangers' who cared less about the men than their own privileges.[12] In thrall to a 'caste creed' inculcated at public school and Sandhurst, they

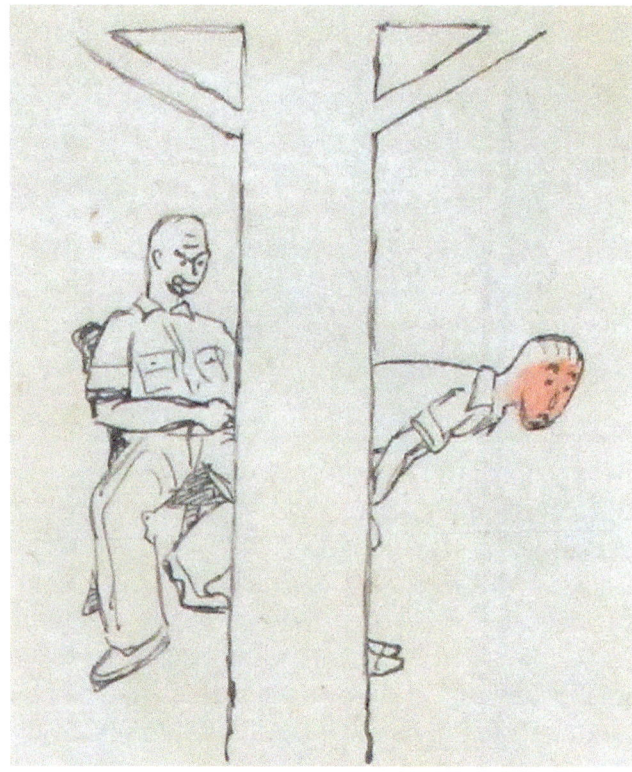

Officer undergoing rectal examination before boarding the *Fukai Maru* (*NIB*)

Officers in the concert room, Christmas 1942. Col. Elrington and Capt. Paque are in the middle of the fourth row. My father is fourth from left, second row

expected to be exempted from work, to eat and sleep apart from their men, and even to have separate toilets. Entitlement in such circumstances cried out to be ridiculed. One British corporal at Changi recalled how the men subverted the officers by deciding that 'everyone would salute everyone. We have great fun. The officers do not approve.'[13] Before the Loyals boarded the *Fukai Maru* in Singapore, the battalion was lined up on the dockside and everyone, up to and including the Governor of the Straits Settlements, was obliged to undergo a public rectal examination with a 'sleek glass rod' to test for diseases. 'This occasioned much embarrassment for the officers,' said Sgt Swarbrick, 'and not a little amusement for the other ranks.'[14]

On Christmas Day 1942, by which time the POWs had been at Keijo for three months, a member of the *Kempeitai* took a photograph of the forty-eight officers of the Loyals and other units in the concert room at Keijo, apparently to be used for propaganda purposes. Despite the austere setting, they appear healthy and well-kempt. One or two are even smiling, or at least trying to.

These were the men for whom *Nor Iron Bars* was produced. It was a magazine by officers, for officers, about officers, and everything about it – the literary references, the classical allusions, the anecdotes about pre-war hunting and shooting parties, the regular columns of bridge problems – proclaims its presumption not just of a certain level but of a certain type of upbringing and education. The other ranks barely feature in its pages. Eight of the Loyals died during the battalion's first three months in Korea, but the Christmas 1942 issue was dedicated to the memory of just one of them, Capt. Jack Whiting.[15]

It was the officers' mess which constituted the world of *Nor Iron Bars*. The only other ranks permitted to enter it were their batmen, a role not always willingly assumed. When John Lever's batman ('Robinson, a young fellow from Wigan') left in July 1944, he had to make do with 'a half share in a new batman, Pledge, but as he was too shy to come into the officers' mess himself, Bombardier Butler collected dirty pots, washing etc. We got another batman after about a week, Caldwell, a more satisfactory individual altogether.' However, Lever had to 'do a bit of my own washing occasionally, as my batman doesn't have much spare time, having to work every day'.[16] Lever often gives the impression that he considered himself rather over-qualified for the role of POW.

The question of whether officers could be obliged to work was never easily resolved. At some camps, the Japanese made them join their men for a few days but, having established the principle, then dropped the matter.[17] At Keijo, one or two officers accompanied every working-party that left the camp, but not to work. Their role was to maintain discipline and try to resolve disputes between the men and the guards. This was a miserable experience, said Lever, just hanging about in sub-zero temperatures all day, eating food that had gone cold, but 'thank God I am not one of the troops who have to go out every day to do work fit only for coolies.'[18] Working parties went out almost daily, winter or summer, to a variety of locations. The most gruelling and dangerous task was levelling a site for a new factory. A cliff wall had to be undermined and the stone broken up, shovelled into trucks and pushed several hundred yards along a rudimentary track. Accidents were common, and two prisoners died. The POWs also had to construct the bed for a new railroad track to run down to the river. At the military warehouse, they were employed almost continuously throughout their time at Keijo carrying sacks of grain, some of them weighing nearly a hundred kilos, or untying knots in rice-ropes and sorting them into bundles. 'Knots' was a particularly cold and unpleasant job, since they could not move around or wear gloves. Other working locations included a farm two miles outside the city and the warehouse at the railway station, where they loaded or unloaded sacks, crates or timber. Although heavy work, this had its compensations, not just because of the opportunities to pilfer food but also because the men enjoyed changing the destination labels on goods in order to 'upset the Japs' calculations'. This was a game which the officers could join: Henling Wade recalled one occasion at the station warehouse when he found a generator labelled for Manchuria and redirected it to Tokyo.[19] There was also occasional work to be done for civilian contractors, where the food, pay and conditions all tended to be better, although jobs did not usually last very long.

Working-party at Keijo railway station (*SPK*)

It may be that Wade, having once been a private himself, formed a closer bond with the other ranks than most of his fellow officers. He found American and Australian officers to be more approachable than the British: they had a 'genuine comradeship' with their men. They slept and ate with their troops, shared their rations, and interceded for them with the Japanese. Their reward, he wrote, was to earn the men's respect, whereas British military tradition had a tendency to 'deepen the gulf' between ranks, so that a lot of British troops despised their officers.[20] Obviously this was not true of all British officers: Col. Philip Toosey, from the Wirral, the Allied commanding officer at Tamarkan camp on the Burma–Thailand railway who was so grotesquely lampooned in *The Bridge on the River Kwai*, earned enormous respect from his men for his willingness to challenge the Japanese and refusal to allow the officers there to segregate themselves. So did the Ulsterman Col. Francis Dillon, senior commander at Sonkurai, 150 miles further north. But along with the care which they and many others showed for their men, what characterised the leadership of Toosey and Dillon was the strict discipline they imposed. 'Men without officers are dead men', said Dillon, and therein lay the crux of the matter.[21] Whatever they thought of certain individuals, or even of the breed as a whole, the men needed their officers. Without discipline or leadership, they would be at the mercy of the Japanese.

Meanwhile, the officers faced their own problems, for while the Japanese relied on them to enforce their commands, they simultaneously enjoyed humiliating them in front of their men. Officers needed to act as their men's shock absorbers – sometimes literally. Time and again, officers who stood up to the Japanese – by refusing to allow sick men to be made to work, or standing over a man to try to halt a beating – found themselves slapped or kicked instead. It was the admiration they thereby earned which enabled them to insist upon the discipline and cohesion that maintained self-respect and saved many lives. If discipline broke down, only self-interest remained, a recipe for disintegration, disease and death, as happened at camps where officers did not show leadership.

Officers at Keijo seldom faced the almost daily life-and-death dilemmas of the railway, but acting as a buffer for the men still involved tricky decisions. One day in early April 1944 when Lever was supervising a working-party at the warehouse, a private who was caught helping himself to a handful of peas was given 'a couple of hearty smacks across the face' by the sentries, then brought to him for a dressing-down: 'As they understood practically no English I told the fellow we must make it look as if I was giving him a good choking off, then they would be satisfied and drop the matter.' However, the man insisted on telling his side of the story. When Lever heard this, it initially seemed to him that the sentries had acted so precipitately that he should submit a formal complaint, but when the Korean foreman who had reported the incident was summoned to give his version of the story, it soon became obvious that the POW was telling 'as plain as daylight, a pack of lies', which 'would have made me look a fool if I had taken it up with the authorities'. Had the man simply apologised, 'they would have dropped the matter immediately', but he continued to lie until another sentry lost patience and 'gave him quite a good bashing'. Fortunately, Lever was able to 'fix it up with the sentries' to draw a line under the incident: 'Had the matter gone to the office, the bloke would very likely have got another bashing there.'[22]

Most of the officers at Keijo supervised at most one working-party each week, but the penalty they paid was a sense of weightless boredom. 'My daily routine is more or less as follows,' wrote Lever in February 1943: 'Reveille and Roll-Call 7.00. Breakfast 7.30. Bridge Lessons 11–12. Lunch 12. P.T. and volleyball 2–3. Japanese Lessons 3–4 Tues and Fri. Supper 5.45. Malay Lessons 6.30–7.30 Mon, Wed and Fri. Roll-Call 8.00. Lights Out 9.00. Out with working party about once a fortnight.'[23] Endless rubbers of bridge provided some relief, but even fanatics discovered their limit and it was eventually superseded by mah-jong. Lever played mah-jong 'practically every afternoon' during October 1944.[24] He also read over a hundred of the books provided by the ICRC or the YMCA, mostly fiction but also philosophy, history, religion, biography and manuals on agriculture and economics. French, German, Spanish or Malay language lessons provided further mental stimulation, while a new camp interpreter, 'Professor' Ukai, offered 'excellent instruction' in Japanese. There were also English literature classes, Shakespeare play-readings, chess competitions and of course *Nor*

Iron Bars.²⁵ Several officers sketched or painted, some of them very well. For exercise, volleyball was always popular, and a ping-pong table purchased in April 1943 led to a series of tournaments between officers and men.²⁶ Highland dancing lessons were given by two of the Scottish officers, until banned. Two or three times a month one of the officers (or occasionally a sergeant or a private) would give a lecture, usually about a military campaign, pre-war occupations, or places they had visited, until in May 1943 Ukai attended a lecture by Col. Elrington on the duke of Marlborough and discovered that one of the duke's descendants was Winston Churchill, whereupon lectures were banned. It made little difference: from now on they were simply referred to as 'Thinking aloud'.²⁷ There was also a camp choir, a 'troops band' which occasionally performed in the officers' mess, an officers' band, and a regular programme of keenly-anticipated concerts organised by Jack McNaughton and usually starring Gloria d'Earie. Unfortunately, McNaughton and several of the camp's musicians (though not Gloria) were transferred to Japan in late 1943, leaving only a 'squeeze-box' for music. However, the concerts continued.²⁸

It is difficult to know what the other ranks at Keijo thought of their officers. The officers themselves complained to the ICRC

Capt. Jack McNaughton as a cheecha (lizard), one of many caricatures of officers as 'insect life' or 'bird life' to appear in *Nor Iron Bars*. Note the reference to his leading 'lady', Gloria d'Earie. 'Tid'apa' was Malay for 'no worries' (*NIB*)

representatives that, as well as their deliberate humiliation by some of the guards, the fact that they lived at such close quarters with their men led to a loss of respect. The high proportion of officers in Keijo also made their insistence on special treatment seem rather anomalous and their relative lack of hardship more conspicuous.[29] Yet it is hard to find expressions of antipathy towards them. The sketchbook published by Toze and Strange in 1947 mentions Col. Elrington and Maj. Lyddon in favourable terms, although without going into detail. Sgt Swarbrick certainly admired Elrington, and thought Maj. Barnes was 'a damn good bloke'. Swarbrick spent most of his captivity at Jinsen, where the officers were known as 'The Puppet Government', but that did not mean that they were disliked, for although they had lost the trust of the men at Singapore, he added that they subsequently regained it, partly by standing up for them against the Japanese and partly by using their own money to buy drugs and other medical supplies for their men. According to Lever, the officers at Keijo did likewise, often passing on some of their wages – although 'surreptitiously', since the Japanese made them account for what they spent – while a rather enigmatic poem in *Nor Iron Bars* claimed that they 'often gave away their stew'. Apart from food, what the men craved was cigarettes, but they were paid so little (three yen a month, compared to the officers' fifty yen) that they could only buy three packs a week, so the officers also gave them extra 'smokos'.[30]

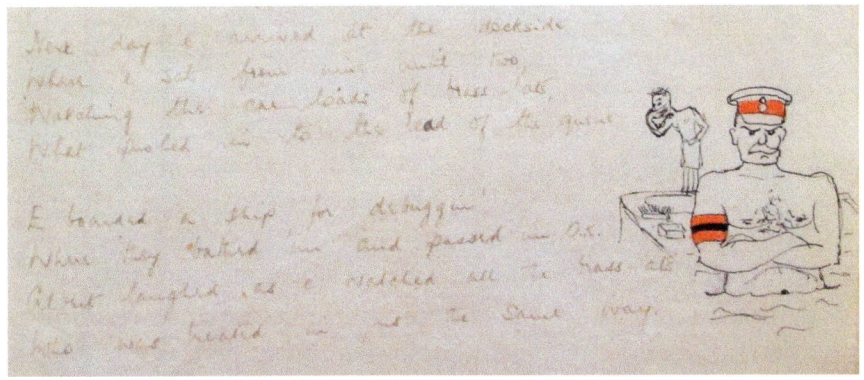

The 'Brass Hats' from the viewpoint of 'Albert' (*NIB*)

The Australian POWs at Keijo were predictably more forthright in their views. A seasonal greeting from 'the Aussies' which appeared in the Christmas 1944 issue of *Nor Iron Bars* was addressed jointly to the 'Bah Goom, where's mah booter' boys and the 'My dear old chappie' boys. The previous year, an article entitled 'The Bushwhacker' had pointed out that in the circumstances in which they currently found themselves, 'a man must be possessed of considerable education, though not of the kind that one would receive at Eton and Harrow'. The 'bushman,' it went on, had learned 'the means of meeting and overcoming material and circumstantial difficulties which will be encountered many times in his everyday existence', and 'city-dwellers whose minds are mainly engrossed in the matching of shirts and ties, tram fares and the latest fashions might well compare the ways of these bushmen to their own'.[31]

Arguably the greatest contribution which most of the officers made to the wellbeing of the camp as a whole was their vegetable garden. They first raised this idea soon after their arrival at Keijo, and Noguchi was more than willing to facilitate it: free vegetables would save him money, and in return he promised them more fish or meat. A two-acre plot was found at a former cavalry depot about a mile from the camp, tools were provided by the YMCA, a thousand tomato plants were purchased by the officers, and on 24 March 1943 the first officer working-party began constructing drainage and embankments. By mid-July, 2,000 kilos of tomatoes and sacks full of potatoes, cabbages, leeks, carrots, maize, spinach, *daikon*, cucumber, lettuce, onions, aubergines, pumpkins and melons were being carried back to the camp cookhouse on an almost daily basis to enrich and vitaminize the soups and stews of both officers and other ranks. An added incentive for the gardeners was that they could fill their bellies with raw vegetables as they worked. Although not very appetizing, 'it makes you feel so full having a decent amount of food for a change'.[32] For some of them, gardening would become something of an obsession. 'No small farm was ever so carefully planned and tilled,' wrote Wade. 'It became a model farm, and Korean farmers would squat on their haunches on the embankments which surrounded it, watching

The officers' first garden at Keijo (*IDS*)

our activities and techniques.'³³ As soon as practicable after the winter, in mid-March 1944, planting began once more.

Naturally Japanese support for the garden was not entirely disinterested. Lt Terada – who, as a graduate of Agricultural College, took a keen though not always welcome interest in it – told the POWs they must also grow castor oil plants there, to provide lubricating oil for machinery. The officers duly complied, but some 'well-planned sabotage' meant that very little castor oil was produced. Unfortunately, the site was also liable to flooding, and in late July 1944 several days of heavy rain left much of the tomato crop suitable only for jam. Even so, more than 2,500 kilos of carrots and potatoes alone were harvested by late October. By this time the officers had also progressed to animal husbandry, since in September 1944 two pigs arrived at the camp, Maud and Mary. Cpl Bromley was appointed as their batman and they soon put on weight, but 'whether we shall be eating them for Christmas remains to be seen'.

It was the proverbially rampant proliferation of the rabbit population which saved them. Soon after the Loyals arrived at Keijo, one of the sergeants had been given a buck rabbit and three does. Two years later, their progeny had grown to around two hundred, although the paterfamilias had died of overexertion after being left too long with the does. It was rabbit pie, therefore, not pork chops, that was on the menu for Christmas dinner, and Maud and Mary were reprieved. By early January 1945 another four pigs had arrived, Monty, Margaret, Micky and Minnie, and on 14 April Maud gave birth to four piglets, Myrtle, Maurice, Melvyn and Martin. By June there were thirteen, but for four of them the

89

Maud and Mary in the pen built for them in the camp exercise yard. If water was spilt in the squad rooms it would flood the floor below, whose occupants would call 'Come down and mop it up' (*NIB*, Christmas 1944)

reprieve proved temporary as they provided a celebratory feast a few days after the war ended.[34] As for the garden, the railroad authorities in Keijo announced in the autumn of 1944 that they were requisitioning the land. A new site was found, and although it was nearly three miles from the camp, the officers continued to work there until the day Japan surrendered.

One of Keijo's doe rabbits asks the buck whether tomorrow might be declared a yasume (holiday) from his attentions (*NIB*)

PRISONER STORIES

Artists

For several of the prisoners, their preferred source of solace was to paint or draw. As with so much prisoner art through the ages, it provided an outlet for their resentment and a little nourishment for the soul. Some of them had brought water-colour sets from Singapore, others improvised, fashioning brushes from coconut fibres or their own hair and pigments from plants and roots, clay and soot. On the whole, however, POWs drew rather than painted, using paper ripped from books, re-used from old messaging pads or surreptitiously purchased from Koreans in return for chewing gum or cigarettes.

Sketches or paintings by at least seven Keijo POWs have survived. They include two of the editors of *Nor Iron Bars* (Henling Wade and my father), Bdr Alan Toze, Sgt S. Strange and the AIF Cpl John Wilkinson. However, the camp's two outstanding artists, both Loyals, were Capt. Donald Teale and Pte Harry Kingsley. Commissioned in June 1940, Teale served as intelligence officer at Singapore command headquarters during the Japanese invasion of the island, but re-joined the Loyals at Changi a month after the capitulation. Like most of the battalion's officers, he remained at Keijo for the full three years, where he produced a number of pencil-portraits of his fellow officers. Only a few of these survive, but those which

Pencil portrait by Donald Teale of an unidentified officer, Keijo, June 1944

Donald Teale, pencil self-portrait, August 1944

do are images of real quality, not just excellent likenesses but fizzing with depth and character. He also drew a gimlet-eyed self-portrait dated 15 August 1944. Teale was also a talented actor and an excellent, witty cartoonist, responsible for many of the best cartoons to appear in *Nor Iron Bars*. Recognisable by their bold but simple lines, they are notable for their sharp humour, expressive body poses and spare but effective use of shading.

Cartoon by Donald Teale (*NIB*, Easter 1945)

Madame Butterfly and Mount Fuji, probably by John Wilkinson
(*NIB*, January 1943)

Apart from Teale, it is not easy to identify the authors of most of the illustrations in *Nor Iron Bars*. John Wilkinson's principal artistic legacy from Keijo is the booklet, *Sketches of a POW in Korea*, which he dedicated to his friend Corporal Reg Hayter of Sydney, who died in captivity. It is set out in story-board format with captions describing the experiences of the Australian and other prisoners at Keijo and then Jinsen. These are in black and white, but Wilkinson also tried his hand at painting in the Japanese style, producing a few delicately-toned and restful landscapes, some but not all of which he signed.

Like Wilkinson, Toze and Strange also published a booklet of sketches after the war, *In Defence of Singapore*, but do not seem to have contributed to *Nor Iron Bars*. Nor did Pte Harry Kingsley. Born in Manchester in 1914, Kingsley enlisted in 1933 and remained with the Loyals until 1946. His leg was crushed in

Harry Kingsley before the war

Le Singerie (the 'Monkey Trick'). Harry Kingsley sketching Dr O'Donnell, the senior Allied medical officer at Keijo. Note the bandaged leg after his accident (IWM)

a working-party accident in November 1942 and he limped for the remainder of his life, but at least this gave him more time to draw, as he was often excused work. Several hundred of his pencil sketches survive. Like Teale, he had a talent for authentic likenesses, but his work had a whimsical element about it. His subjects are restless, and he liked to depict himself as a monkey (he was five feet five inches tall). Yet his draughtsmanship is beyond doubt. After the war Kingsley studied at Manchester School of Art, where he learned to paint Lowry-like industrial townscapes and evocative landscapes in bold colour-blocks, quite unlike his work at Keijo. He died in 1998, but his POW drawings were still being exhibited at the Museum of Lancashire in 2005.

Henling Wade and my father also contributed illustrations to *Nor Iron Bars*, mostly humorous caricatures of POWs or camp officials as birds or insects, spindly pen or pencil sketches of life at Keijo, wistful 'advertisements' for home comforts, or magazine issue covers. Only occasionally, however, is it possible to identify the artist of an individual drawing, as in the following example of a signed preliminary sketch by my father for a caricature of Jiminy Paque which appeared in *Nor Iron Bars*.

Sketch of Jiminy Paque signed PGW (my father)

SIX

Mainichi

WHEN THE LOYALS ARRIVED AT KEIJO in September 1942, World War II stood at a crossroads. Two months later it turned. On 11 November, Allied victory at the second battle of El Alamein halted the Axis advance towards the Suez Canal and the Middle Eastern oilfields; on 15 November, Japanese progress in the South Pacific was brought to a shattering halt at the Naval Battle of Guadalcanal (Solomon Islands); and on 19 November, the Russians launched Operation Uranus, leading within four days to the encirclement of the German sixth army at Stalingrad. By mid-February 1943, the sixth army had surrendered, Japan had abandoned Guadalcanal and Rommel's *Africa Korps* had been driven out of Egypt and Libya. Hearing of the American victory at Guadalcanal, President Roosevelt commented, 'It appears that the turning point in this war has at last been reached.' Although not yet setting, the Rising Sun had passed its zenith. Allied optimism in Europe, although cautious at first – 'this is not even the beginning of the end,' Churchill famously warned, 'but it is, perhaps, the end of the beginning' – was also justified.

Apart from food, there was nothing POWs craved more than news about the war. When the editors of *Nor Iron Bars* asked their readers what they would spend one shilling on if they could have anything they wanted, the answers divided equally between 'a decent meal' and an up-to-date British newspaper (preferably the *Times* or *Telegraph*).[1] At some Japanese camps, desperation drove the prisoners to build clandestine radios ('canaries'), but discovery meant a vicious beating at best and at worst beheading.[2] A dramatized account of a discussion in the officers' mess at Keijo implies that a few weeks after their arrival they debated whether

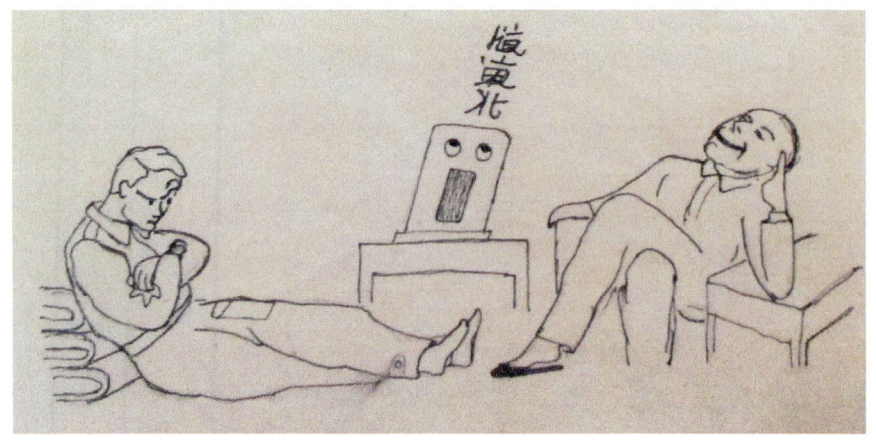

Imagining the pleasure of having a wireless (*NIB*)

to ask Noguchi if he would give them a radio. The general opinion was that in the unlikely event that he agreed, it probably wouldn't work. Two of the officers claimed to know how to build one, but there is no indication that they did.³

Instead, they had to rely on what little they were told by the guards, the scraps they could glean from sympathetic Koreans while out on working-parties, and what they were allowed to read. Each of these sources was incomplete and unreliable. A few days after arriving at Keijo, the POWs were told that Stalingrad had fallen to the Germans and Rommel was within touching distance of Alexandria. It was 'the lowest ebb of the war', and it was five months before they learned the truth.⁴ Their main source of news at this time was the *Japan Times*, a weekly English-language magazine produced in Tokyo which Noguchi hoped would encourage them to see the war from a different perspective, although the copies they received were usually about a fortnight out of date. More satisfactory was *Mainichi* ('Every Day'), an Osaka-based newspaper, also published in English, which they began receiving in early March 1943. As its name suggests, it was printed daily and usually reached the POWs within forty-eight hours.⁵ Although *Mainichi* was naturally filtered through chrysanthemum-tinted spectacles, the POWs soon learned to decode the 'facts' it presented. Thus when Axis forces were said to be 'holding their positions', or 'making adjustments', or 'operating in a new sphere', it almost invariably meant that they were retreating. Half-remembered geography also helped. By mid-March 1943, fighting on Europe's Eastern Front was reported in the Donetsk region of Ukraine, along the Kharkiv-Rostov-Novorossiysk line, three hundred miles or more west of Stalingrad – a measure of how far the Red Army had advanced in six weeks. Careful scrutiny of half-buried news items could also be rewarding: thus 'it suddenly came to light that Rangoon had been air-raided almost daily for months', or that air-raid shelters were being built in Tokyo. 'The Japs are not very good propagandists and don't profess to be as good at it as we are', wrote Lever.[6]

Japanese claims of the number of Allied ships 'sunk' or planes 'shot down' were particularly suspect. Following one American air-raid, *Mainichi* announced that 201 out of 270 bombers had been destroyed – a manifestly ludicrous claim. 'Pessimists divided all claims by four and believed the result; the optimists believed nothing,' wrote Henling Wade. The truth, always a moving target,

Cartoon celebrating the news of the Battle of El Alamein (*NIB*)

at times vanished entirely. On one occasion it was said that a Japanese pilot, a 'Hero-God', having run out of ammunition, brought down an American plane with his sword.[7] Yet once they had learned the code, the POWs were able to keep themselves broadly up to date with the war, and everything they heard, from Italy to North Africa to the Eastern Front to Burma to the Pacific, told the same story, of Allied advance and Axis retreat. Diplomatic and political developments were similarly encouraging. The conference between Churchill and Roosevelt at Casablanca (14–24 January 1943), Churchill's follow-up visit to Turkey (which 'might come in on our side'), the Washington conference in May, the downfall of Mussolini on 25 July and the Tehran and Cairo summits of late November–early December were all known about in Keijo within a month.[8] Particular attention was paid to the fighting in North Africa and Italy, since the 1st Loyals' Battalion took part in both campaigns. Indeed it was highly probable, wrote Col. Elrington in the July 1943 issue of *Nor Iron Bars*, that the 1st Loyals were at that very moment fighting in the vicinity of Maida

News as it appeared in Japanese newspapers (*NIB*)

As the war turned against Japan, more and more news was cut out of the *Japan Times* (*NIB*)

(Calabria), where in 1806 the 81st Foot (later the Loyals) had helped secure a famous victory against Napoleon's forces, an engagement still commemorated on the regimental colours.[9]

With such relentlessly good news, it was easy to get carried away. As early as April 1943, *Nor Iron Bars* was claiming that the war in Europe was 'in the bag' and 'the final Allied push cannot be far off'.[10] The despondency of 1942 gave way to triumphalism:

> Britannia now rides forth again, her shield and trident strong,
> And bloody tyrants squeal in vain, who sought to do her wrong,
> So must we captives here, all chance of fighting thus denied,
> Forget complacent arrogance, but not our rightful pride.[11]

By Christmas 1943, the editors felt confident enough to announce that this would be the penultimate issue of *Nor Iron Bars*. The final issue would commemorate the Allied victory, a 'bumper number' to which everyone was invited to contribute. Nor should they wait too long, since the war might end even sooner than expected.¹² Yet one question troubled them: when would the long-awaited Second Front be opened? Churchill had expressed the hope in July that the Allies would invade France 'when autumn leaves are falling', and that once Germany and Italy were crushed all available resources would be poured into the war against Japan. Stalin, desperate to relieve the pressure on the Red Army, continually urged Britain and America to act, but as autumn turned to winter it became clear that this would not happen before next spring at the earliest.¹³ The editors of *Nor Iron Bars* duly apologised in April 1944 for the wave of optimism that had overtaken them during 1943: 'now, though we are no less optimistic and our confidence no wit diminished, we anticipate a few more months of captivity and a new lease of life for *Nor Iron Bars*'. But they would make no further predictions as to how long that might last.¹⁴

As Japan's difficulties mounted, the prisoners' access to news was steadily cut back. At the end of October 1943, daily issues of *Mainichi* suddenly ceased. They were still given the *Japan Times* once a fortnight, but by March 1944 reports of the war in Burma and the Pacific were being cut out of it. On 9 June, however, three days after D-Day, this too was stopped (although not before they had heard of the Normandy landings).¹⁵

From now on, the POWs had only Japanese-language sources to rely on. Korean sentries or civilians would slip them copies of two or three-day-old newspapers, and after a few months they managed to recruit a young Korean boy who, in return for cigarettes or chewing gum from Red Cross parcels, would pass by the officers' garden each day and slip a local newspaper through a sliding panel at the back of the shed. Brought back to camp in a false sleeve sewn to the inside of a webbing belt, this would be translated by the polyglot Lt George Baker of the Loyals, who had assiduously attended Professor Ukai's Japanese lessons. As a result, 'we have hardly missed a day's news'.¹⁶ Yet it still took a good deal of unearthing, for, as a contributor to the Christmas 1944 issue of *Nor Iron Bars* put it, 'the Nipponese buries his words in a very labyrinth of references and cross-references, bristling menacingly with wriggling movements'. Patience was needed: two hieroglyphs, for 'Tokyo' and 'Air-raid', were easy enough to identify, but only when a third eventually yielded itself to scrutiny did the true significance of the headline become apparent: 'Tokyo Repeatedly Raided! Voilà tout!'[17]

A month later, the evidence of news reports was supplemented by that of the prisoners' eyes and ears, for at 10.30 on the morning of 18 January 1945 the first American B-29 Superfortress was seen above Keijo. The joy of the moment is captured in both the cover image of the next *NIB*, which featured a B-29, and a poem, 'We Waited Three Years':

> The sound grows deeper, till high up above
> Appears a glittering white and silver dove,
> With wings outstretched, so high it seems to hover
> Blazing a four-streamed misty vaporous trail,
> As though to scorn the feeble frantic fire
> With all its grace and strength. Our hearts aspire
> To thoughts of freedom's herald, and we hail
> Thee, friend, serenely sailing, westward bent.
> Return in scores! With bombs your vengeance vent![18]

Twelve days later another B-29 appeared, and soon the POWs were put to work constructing an underground food store and slit trenches in the exercise yard. By the time the final issue of *Nor Iron Bars* appeared on 1 April, air-raid sirens were sounding and the crump of distant bombs punctuated the hours. 'Germany must soon be crushed,' wrote Lever, 'then Japan will have her time either to be crushed or to throw her hand in. Whichever way they choose, we can wait.'[19]

It was advisable not to wait too long, however, because as the inevitability of Japanese humiliation loomed, relations between the prisoners and their captors became increasingly edgy. 'The sentries have been more troublesome lately,' wrote Lever, 'and the Japanese generally'.[20] Petty restrictions and acts of retribution multiplied. Letters from home, always so eagerly-awaited by POWs, were held in the office for weeks or even months before being handed out. Visits to the officers' garden were strictly monitored. Even gazing out of the windows of the squad-rooms

Cover image of *Nor Iron Bars*, Easter 1945

was prohibited – the sentries found it disconcerting. Stoves were removed from the rooms on 1 March, two or three weeks earlier than usual despite the intense cold, and the permitted hours of electric lighting were curtailed,[21] while snap roll-calls and searches became more frequent. One of these almost led to the detection of the latest issue of *Nor Iron Bars*, but it was quickly stuffed in a pile of clothing.

Yet far from cowing the prisoners, this only seems to have goaded them into further defiance. As early as March 1944, when they were asked to fill in questionnaires giving their opinions about the Japanese army and the progress of the war, 'the replies were quite direct, no effort was made to be complimentary'. Even more direct was their reaction to one of Terada's less welcome visits to the officers' mess one night in the spring of 1944, colourfully evoked in *Nor Iron Bars*.[22] It was long after lights out, when 'rhythmic breathing broken only by the occasional raspberry of escaping flatus broke the silence'. Suddenly, with 'a clatter of sword and boots', Terada and the interpreter Ushihara marched into the room, switched the lights on and ordered the men out of bed. A 'low growl of hatred' went around the room at the sight of Terada's 'fat, podgy face spasmodically diffused with purple mottling, like an excited turkey cock', while Ushihara, 'small, yellow and insignificant, tried to assimilate some of the wrath of his senior officer'. Waving a memorandum, Terada shouted that some sugar had been pilfered from the store, and 'you officers must prevent these things happening!'

Jiminy Paque, still in his pyjamas and looking like 'an angry sea-lion just roused from sleep', reached for his instruction booklet and 'snarled' at Ushihara: 'You show me where you have issued any instructions.'

'No. You show me,' replied Ushihara, pointing out (irrelevantly) that the booklet was undated.

'Whose bloody book is it anyway?' retorted Paque.

Col. Elrington, towering above them, stood by in his pyjamas looking 'faintly amused', while Capt. Frank Beattie, at no pains to hide his disdain, lay back on his mat and starting reading a novel.

With 'audible encouragement coming from every corner of the delighted room', Ushihara tried to save face by barking, 'You will date your book!' but Paque now had the bit between his teeth.

'Who the hell do you think you are to give me orders?'

Terada, who 'was going from purple to puce and in imminent danger of apoplexy', seized the memorandum, tore it to shreds and, 'raising the fragments aloft in clenched fist he hurled them to the floor with a final howl of "Lies!", before wheeling and, with clank of sword, striding from the room, with Ushihara almost trotting to keep up'. 'A gust of laughter from the whole room' followed them down the stairs, and in due course the lights were turned off and everyone tried to go back to sleep.

It was not just the POWs who were rattling their cages at the prospect of imminent liberation. Korea had been under what was by any standards a brutal Japanese occupation since 1910, and during the war thousands of Koreans were press-ganged into service either as prison-camp guards, where they were treated little better than the POWs, or as 'comfort women', who were treated a good deal worse. (It has been estimated that three of every four comfort women died.) As the day of liberation approached, some of them became less inclined to hide their feelings. Now, when the POWs were marched or driven through Keijo on working-parties, the Koreans in the streets began cheering them, despite the presence of Japanese guards. However, they still had to be careful. In May 1945, after Germany's surrender, one of the Korean guards at Keijo was overheard making an anti-Japanese speech while out enjoying a night in the town. He was 'badly beaten up' and taken

Christmas 1944: cover of *Nor Iron Bars*

away by the *Kempeitai*.²³ Not until Japan finally acknowledged defeat would its grip loosen.

Paradoxically, Col. Noguchi appears to have become more amenable during the last months of the war, perhaps because he was better informed than his underlings and understood that the game truly was up. For Christmas 1944, each man was given a whole Red Cross parcel and the POWs enjoyed 'the best meal we have had for three years'. Lunch consisted of rabbit pie or stew, salmon *au gratin*, a loaf of bread, a whole tin of bully beef each and even a bottle of beer (although 'a brand that fellows wouldn't drink in Shanghai in peacetime'). In the afternoon 'Paddy Given-Wilson and John Turner got up a good treasure hunt' followed by a concert starring Gloria d'Earie and a supper of bully beef rissoles, tinned fish, cake with chocolate sauce, coffee and apple brandy. 'We were a happy crowd together,' said Lever – not least because they knew that this would almost certainly be their last Christmas in captivity.²⁴

Noguchi also allowed the POWs to send additional postcards home (although naturally these were still censored) and in January 1945 they were even permitted to send one (vetted) telegram each. A month later all the remaining Red Cross parcels were handed over to Col. Elrington with permission for the POWs to distribute

Paper for rolling cigarettes was often in short supply (*NIB*)

them as they wished. As their diet improved, they began to put on weight again, although the highly-prized Chesterfield cigarettes continued to be a source of anxiety. For most of their time at Keijo the prisoners had been issued with ten cigarettes a day, but in March 1945 this was scaled down to forty-five a week, and in June to just a hundred a month. With every butt-end scrupulously recycled, the exercise-yard had never looked tidier. It was the supply of books, the chief source of cigarette paper, which was in greater danger of running out.

Ever since the early days of their captivity, the POWs had looked forward to the day of liberation with a mixture of yearning and trepidation. The yearning, which requires no explanation, was expressed in numerous articles and poems in *Nor Iron Bars* with titles such as 'Be it Soon!' or 'I'd rather live in England in the rain', often accompanied by sketches of idealized pastoral scenes or the home hearth.[25] The trepidation arose in part from the shame felt by almost all those who had suffered the humiliations of the Malayan Campaign. Shortly after Singapore surrendered, while they were still in Changi, a joke had gone around that if medals were to be awarded for the campaign they would have to be white with a yellow streak.[26] As the prospect of returning to face family and friends approached, apprehension grew. 'I can hear their cheerful voices, they're calling from afar', went a pastiche of Rudyard Kipling's *The Mother Lodge*, 'Come back, you

Dreaming of returning home (*NIB*)

phoney soldier, you've done better in the past/It's a lousy part you're playing and I think you've been miscast'.²⁷ After the war, advised a contributor to the final issue, it might be better 'to leave false clues about one's movements about the world' rather than to 'reveal beyond question that one is a member of the Malayan Civil Service, an officer in the Indian army, an ex-prisoner of Japan, or otherwise untouchable'.²⁸

Equally unsettling was the question of whether the POWs would be able to adapt to normal life after three and a half years of privation. Would they be too institutionalized, too degraded by the experience? How soon would their stomachs adapt to a Western diet? One of them tried to imagine the sort of letters his wife might write to her friends about him following his return: he greets guests with 'a stiff little bow from the hips', 'crams all his pockets full of match-boxes which he hoards with the joy of a miser', refuses to use any cutlery apart from a little spoon, even at dinner parties, orders turnips and soya-bean sauce for breakfast, and complains loudly in public about his constipation, as a result of which he spends most of his time in what he calls the *banjo* [*sic*], from which he has insisted on removing the seat since he claims that 'the straddle position facilitates unrestrained action

How soon would the POWs adapt to a Western diet? (*NIB*)

without any rupture to the bowel' and is therefore 'the natural opponent of constipation'.²⁹

Others were worried that they might no longer be welcome at their former clubs in St James's Street or the Mall. Fellow members would complain about 'these prison-weary beings who, though revelling in their new-found freedom, had become so accustomed, quite unconsciously, to a dull routine and to unnatural habits that they were totally unable to change their ways'. They shaved in their tea at breakfast, inquired loudly in the dining-room whether anyone wanted the remains of their soup, cleaned their teeth in the urinals, killed off the pot-plants in the card-room by emptying the dregs of their tea-cups into them and continually peered into the ashtrays to see if there were any butt-ends worth saving. Instead of tipping the waiters, they offered them old pieces of clothing. The upshot of 'this disgraceful assault upon the sanctity of English club life' was the inauguration of a new club, 'The Outcasts', membership of which was restricted to 'this heathen community'.³⁰ Another article related how, fifteen years after the war, an unsuspecting rambler in the South Downs stumbled upon a 'queer little colony' called 'Little Keijo sur le Meshi'. Patrolled by 'a police force recruited entirely from the local lunatic asylum', it consisted of a four-storey brick building surrounded by wooden huts. One of the locals told him that it had been set up by people who 'had found everyday English life too much for them', and although there was no compulsion on any of the colonists to remain, those who occasionally tried to break away 'always returned, baffled and bewildered'. On investigation, the rambler found a number of aging figures sitting around dejectedly, constructing pointless piles of clay and coal or lying listlessly on low mat-covered platforms in the dormitory. Others were eating in grim silence, concentrating on their chewing. All around the walls were old crates full of odd pieces of wire or rope, while in one corner two 'furtive-looking individuals' sat at a table, one of them 'hammering with one finger at an incredibly ancient typewriter', while the other, 'who had looked up in a very guilty manner and tried to conceal some papers, now continued to dictate. One muttered to the other "Must get it out by Christmas!"' – a rare glimpse into the making of *Nor Iron Bars*.³¹

"Anybody want my fish?"

How welcome at their clubs would ex-POWs be after liberation? (*NIB*)

What many of the POWs clearly understood was that the challenge would be to prevent three and a half years of bodily imprisonment from becoming the incubator of a lifetime's mental imprisonment, a tiger padding softly behind them as long as they continued to walk this earth. Of more immediate concern, however, were darker fears. Japanese military discipline did not permit surrender: the honourable path was to die fighting. If and when the Japanese government was forced to capitulate, therefore, how would its soldiers react? Would they agree to surrender? And was it true, as rumoured, that they would first shoot all their prisoners? In certain areas – Formosa, Borneo, the mainland of Japan – orders to that effect were later discovered and presented as evidence to the War Crimes Commission. Henling Wade, who ended the war in Naoetsu camp on Honshu island, was told in early August 1945 by one of his guards that if the Americans invaded the mainland, 'If fighting bad – no good – they kill all officers.' That was why tunnels were being dug in the mountains, so that they could be massacred and buried there. Another POW claimed, 'We had been forced to dig a huge pit which was to be our communal grave. Our guards had received orders to shoot us if mainland Japan was invaded.'[32]

In Korea, the immediate threat to the Japanese came not from the Americans but the Russians, who belatedly declared war on Japan on 9 August 1945 and advanced rapidly through Manchuria. Eleven days after Japan capitulated, my father wrote in a letter to his mother that 'if the Russians had got down as far as Keijo we would most likely have been shoved against a wall'.[33] Fortunately these fears were not realized, and although a few Japanese commanders refused to obey the emperor's order to surrender, these were isolated cases. Nevertheless, there were a few tragic and wholly gratuitous postscripts to capitulation: the last recorded execution of Allied POWs was on 27 August, twelve days after the emperor announced the surrender, when thirty men at Ranau in Borneo were massacred.[34]

PRISONER STORIES

'Their Nibs'

Shortly after the Loyals arrived at Changi, 'two young subalterns' asked Henling Wade, who had worked as a reporter in Shanghai before the war, if he would like to help them write a camp magazine. He agreed, and they began talking about what to call it. 'How about "Stone walls do not a prison make"?' he suggested, thinking of Richard Lovelace's *To Althea, from Prison*. But it was the next line, 'Nor iron bars a cage', which they eventually hit upon.[35]

The 'two young subalterns' were John Turner, who had worked with ICI before the war, and my father, an insurance agent. After Wade left Keijo in November 1943, these two continued to produce *Nor Iron Bars* until the war ended. Issues varied in length from sixteen pages (June 1942) to seventy-three (Easter 1945) and totalled 516 pages. Neither the editors nor contributors maintained complete anonymity, but they did for the most part. Each issue began with a brief editorial signed 'Ed.', usually

Sketch by my father of Tom Henling Wade, his fellow editor (*NIB*)

'Their Nibs', pencil sketch by Harry Kingsley, 1944–5

asking for any available paper, reminding readers to be careful in passing it around, soliciting contributions and occasionally commenting on the progress of the war or other current events; apart from the first, each issue concluded with a brief camp diary.

The conditions under which the magazine was produced were always testing. At Changi, a typewriter was available, but the first two issues at Keijo, eighty-four pages in all, were entirely handwritten. In January 1943, however, the editors managed to get hold of another typewriter – presumably from a friendly Korean, although this was not revealed – which they retained until liberation. Paper was an ongoing problem. Most of *Nor Iron Bars* was produced on sheets of naval messaging pads, with illustrations drawn directly on to the page, which must have taken a good deal of layout planning.

'Three things preserve our sanity,' commented a contributor to the April 1943 issue: 'News, profanity and humour'. Although the diary pages contain a valuable journal of life in the camp, it was emphatically not a news magazine; profanity and humour, on the other hand, it provided in abundance. Its staple fare was made up of articles, generally humorous, parodic or nostalgic, but occasionally addressing more serious topics; poems, many of which were adaptations of verses by Shakespeare or Kipling, always a colonial favourite; short one-act plays or operettas, often adapted from Gilbert and Sullivan; mind-puzzles, including a regular two or three pages of bridge problems; and illustrations, mostly cartoons, of which there might be twenty or thirty per issue. As time passed, a growing number of the officers at Keijo

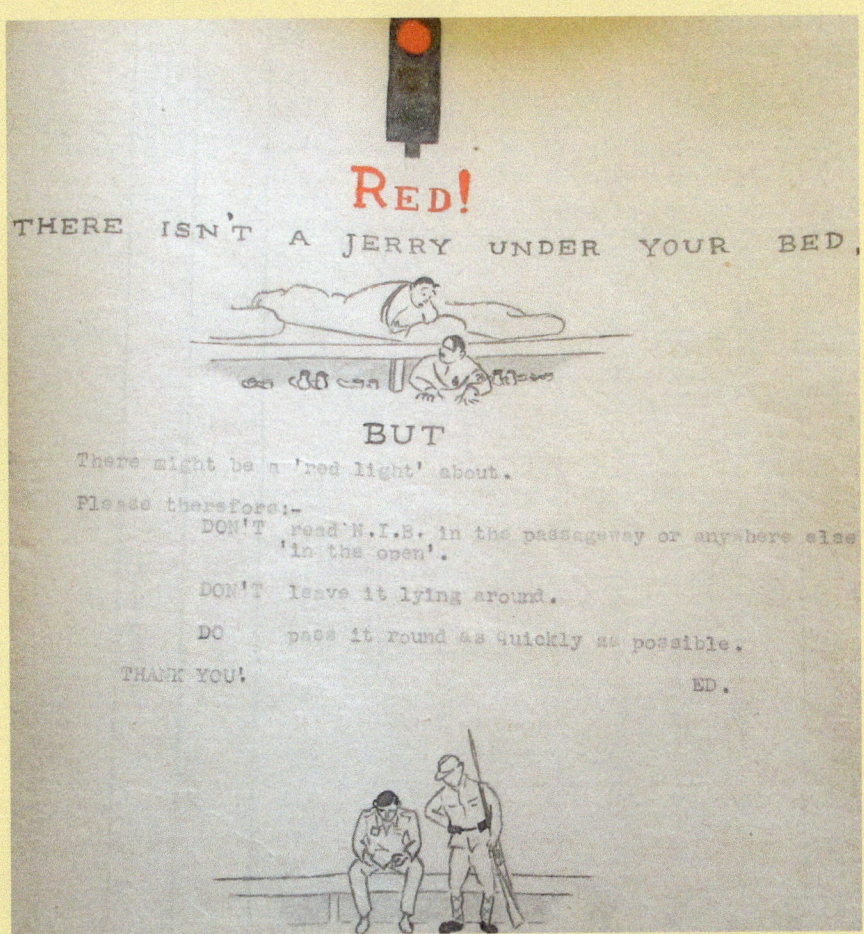

Reminder to readers to be careful. 'Red Light' signalled a prowling sentry (*NIB*)

began contributing, the issues got longer, and the tone of the magazine changed. Readers might think, wrote 'Ed.' in the July 1943 issue, that 'the policy of *Nor Iron Bars* has been changed to one of open hostility towards our present hosts', but this was not the case; it was simply that the contributors' sentiments had hardened and they had grown bolder in expressing them. What lay behind this was doubtless their increasing confidence that their 'hosts' would soon be defeated.

Security was thus crucial. Only one copy of each issue was made, passed from hand to hand and returned to the editors, who hid it in the mess (exactly where is uncertain). In the foreword to the bound volume which Col. Elrington wrote after the war, he stated that 'this constant fear of secrecy added spice to our enjoyment and each successive edition of *Nor Iron Bars* gave a fresh fillip to our morale'. Elrington was a great supporter of the magazine. In April 1943, to mark its first anniversary, he wrote to the editors congratulating them on having given 'great satisfaction to all concerned', urging them to guard the back-numbers carefully and expressing

Imagining the camp officials at Keijo reading *Nor Iron Bars*. Col. Noguchi on the right. The red stamp is a copy of the Japanese censor's stamp, or 'chop' (*NIB*)

the hope that it would 'live after death, as our intention is to have it bound worthily and kept in the officers' mess'.

Col. Elrington was as good as his word. Following liberation, he packed all fourteen issues into his kit and brought them back with him to England, where he added the following foreword:

> To the uninitiated reader, the contents of this quite unique magazine may appear puzzling. He will readily appreciate some of the difficulties that attended its conception, circulation and safe custody; he will perhaps be able to picture the snap inspections of a POW camp, the prying eyes of roving sentries, the stealthy tread of rubber-shod snoopers by day and night. But what he cannot comprehend is the enormity of the disciplinary offences committed by those responsible for NIB, nor the grievous insults to the semi-divine Imperial Majesty of Japan which our innocently irreverent fun constituted in the slanting eyes of our primitive hosts. Offences such as these, believe it or not, were punishable by barbaric torture or death.[36]

Cover board, *Nor Iron Bars*, bound and placed in Lancashire Infantry Museum in 1947

SEVEN

'Not necessarily to Japan's advantage'

When the POWs at Keijo were told that a 'new and most cruel' bomb had been dropped on Hiroshima, and that Russia had entered the war, they knew the end could not be far off. On Monday 13 August, forty or more American fighter-bombers overflew the city, although no bombs were dropped. On the morning of 15 August, a working-party left camp as usual to go to the officers' garden. That afternoon, their regular Korean newspaper boy told them that Japan had surrendered. Having heard several such rumours over the past few weeks, they were sceptical, but later that evening five POWs who had been in the civilian jail walked into the camp after being released, and shortly after this a Korean sentry whispered to a group of officers, 'War over.' That night, they could see bonfires all over the city. Yet still no word came from Col. Noguchi, and next morning the garden party set out again. Crowds of Koreans ran up to them waving copies of the *Korea Times*, giving thumbs up signs and shouting *tomodachi* ('friends'). At first the Japanese guards tried to push them back, but after a while they gave up. On the way home, the streets were thronged with cheering civilians and Korean flags had replaced Japanese. Back at the camp, officials were incinerating documents. Yet still the prisoners were wary. Col. Elrington called a meeting and told them they should remain under camp discipline and avoid any provocation until officially told otherwise. After all, it was still the Japanese who had the guns.

Koreans cheering as the POWs are driven out to work (*IDS*)

As darkness fell on the 16th, the Korean sentries began packing up their bags, and by midnight they were all gone. 'Couldn't sleep last night,' wrote Lever, 'it's the excitement of waiting to be re-born.' At last, on the morning of Friday 17th, Noguchi summoned Elrington to the office and confirmed the news. For the moment, he said, the Japanese guards and officials at Keijo would remain in the camp (partly for their own safety), but all the stores would be handed over to the POWs with immediate effect and there would be no more roll-calls or drills or working-parties. They could smoke or turn lights on or sing or dance or look out of windows whenever they wanted. Soon after this, Lever saw another five POWs arriving from the civilian jail: 'they just walked out, the Koreans were storming around the place all night'. Later two airmen arrived, an American shot down during a bombing raid on the 13th and a Russian who had crashed in the sea on a reconnaissance mission ten days earlier. Both had been kept incommunicado. The American didn't know that the war had ended, while the Russian didn't know that it had begun.[1]

But yes, the war was over. Emperor Hirohito's radio announcement had been made at noon on 15 August, the first time that the semi-divine occupant of the chrysanthemum throne had spoken directly to his people. With a degree of understatement that in less desperate times might almost be mistaken for irony, he told his people that 'despite the best that has been done by everyone, the war situation has developed not necessarily to Japan's advantage', and that the government had decided to accept the terms of the Potsdam Declaration issued by the United States, Britain and China on 26 July. Although the emperor did not use terms such as 'surrender' or 'ceasefire' – too shameful to be spelt out – no one mistook his meaning. The Potsdam Declaration required Japan's immediate and unconditional surrender, the occupation of its homeland, the disarming of its military forces, the renunciation of its conquests and the trials of suspected war criminals. Hirohito himself had been arguing for weeks that the alternative to capitulation was precisely what the Allies said it would be, that is, the 'prompt and utter destruction' of the nation. Yet so deeply was the spirit of *bushido* – the *samurai* code of honour – ingrained in the Japanese character that, even though fifty per cent of Tokyo's buildings had been reduced to rubble, even after 100,000 civilians had been killed in an instant at Hiroshima and Nagasaki, the Japanese cabinet and Supreme Council were still bitterly and more or less evenly divided over whether to surrender or to fight on, and in the end, Hirohito was forced to overrule the dissenters. The whole cabinet promptly resigned, and between the time that he told them of his decision, around midday on 14 August, and his radio broadcast the next day, army minister Anami and around 500 generals and other senior officers committed *hara kiri* rather than witness their country's shame.[2]

For several days after the POWs learned that they were now ex-POWs, little happened. On 20 August Col. Noguchi passed them a message dropped from a B-29. Five days later another message told them that they should alert American pilots by painting PW in large letters on the exercise yard. Four days later supplies were dropped. There was food, clothing, cigarettes and medical supplies – though sadly not in time to save Roger Pigott, who had been brought back to camp on 17th and died on 29 August, the day the first supplies arrived.

```
                ATTENTION
        ALLIED    PRISONERS.

     Allied Prisoners of War and Civilian Internees, these
are your orders and/or instructions in case there is a
capitulation of the Japanese Forces:-

1.   You are to remain in your camp area until you receive
further instructions from this HQ.

2.   Law and order will be maintained in the camp area.

3.   In case of a Japanese surrender there will be Allied
Occupational forces sent into your camp to care for your
needs and eventual evacuation to your homes. You must help
by remaining in the area in which we now know you are located.

4.   Camp leaders are charged with these responsibilities.

5.   The end is near. Do not be disheartened. We are thinking
of you. Plans are under way to assist you at the earliest
possible moment.
                    (Signed)  A.C.Wedemeyer,
                              Lieutenant General, U.S.A.
                              Commanding.

Dropped from U.S. B.729 about 2 p.m. 20/8/45.
```

Leaflet dropped into Keijo Camp, 20 August 1945 (LIM)

By now, said Lever, 'we were getting rather browned off', and tempers in the camp were fraying. One drunken Japanese sergeant with 'a penchant for hitting officers' drew his sword and tried to force his way into the mess, but was pulled away by his colleagues. To defuse the tension, Noguchi organised a visit to the old emperor's palace in Keijo and took a lorryload of his guests for a day out in the countryside, where they went boating and swimming in the Han River. Everywhere they went, there were smiles and handshakes, especially when they handed out the ever-popular packets of chewing gum dropped by the Americans: 'The Allies could have conquered this country with chewing gum if they had known,' wrote Lever. They were also invited to receptions at the Russian consulate in Keijo on 2 September and the French consulate three days later. On 6 September the Roman Catholics among the Loyals (my father included) attended a mass at Keijo cathedral and were introduced to the Bishop of Korea, who escorted them to a local convent for breakfast with the nuns. Before leaving, they all knelt to kiss the bishop's ring, much to the amazement of the Japanese camp officials who had accompanied them, because 'the Koreans have of course been treated like dirt by the Japs, and it was an eye-opener to the Jap officer to see British officers kneeling to a Korean. The Bishop gained a lot of face and was obviously delighted.'[3] This was their last social engagement in Korea. Twenty-four hours later the Americans arrived at Keijo and the POWs began packing up.

Once the fighting stopped, the repatriation of POWs was given the highest priority by Allied command. Within nine days of leaving Keijo by train, the surviving officers and men of the Loyals had been transported via the American hospital ship *Refuge* to Manila in the Philippines, which was 'in a terrible state, all the big buildings burnt out shells and the small buildings for the most part just rubble'. Here they were given thorough medical inspections and interrogated for evidence of Japanese atrocities, later used at the IMT trials. Here too, after three years in their Korean bubble, they met fellow POWs from every part of Japan's ephemeral empire: men who had worked on the Burma–Thailand railway, where 12,000 Allied soldiers (about one in five of those sent there) had died of malnutrition, cholera or simple neglect, along with up to 100,000 native labourers; men who had been put to work in mines or foundries or shipyards in Taiwan or on the Japanese mainland, where some of them had lost half their bodyweight and the death-rate in the worst camps (such as the Kinkaseki copper mine on Taiwan) was over eighty per cent; men who had been in camps in north Borneo, where around 3,200 out of 4,650 POWs died, or the fifty per cent – no more – who had survived imprisonment on Haruku Island (Indonesia), where they had been forced to construct an airfield by 'cutting the tops of hills' using hammers and chisels.[4] Only now did the full truth dawn on the Loyals – namely that, despite the years of incarceration, malnourishment, corporal punishment and degradation they had undergone, Keijo was comparatively speaking one of the best places for prisoners of the Japanese to be held. Compared to what others had suffered, my father wrote to his mother, 'I now realize that we have had an absolute picnic.'⁵

On 25 September 1945, three years and a day since they had stepped ashore in Korea from the *Fukai Maru*, most of the Loyals boarded H.M.S. *Implacable* in Manila to begin their homeward voyage. Built at Govan on the Clyde and only completed in August 1944, the 31,220-ton *Implacable* was the Royal Navy's most up-to-date aircraft carrier. Since joining the British Pacific Fleet in May 1945, its Seafire and Firefly fighter-bomber pilots had (by their own estimation) brought down 113 Japanese aircraft, sunk 148,000 tons of Japanese shipping and flown scores of bombing raids over Japan. Now, having been shorn of much of its firepower during a hasty refit at Sydney, it was to spend the next three months ferrying groups of ex-POWs across the Pacific. The Loyals were in *Implacable*'s first batch of 3,718 troops, mainly Americans and Canadians. Stopping for a day at Pearl Harbor, they reached Vancouver on 11 October, continued by train to Halifax, Nova Scotia, and reached England at the end of October. Most of them had not been home for at least four years, but Henling Wade was disappointed at their reception. Their American liberators had treated them 'like royalty', and all the way across Canada they were 'cheered and honoured' by crowds lining platforms and docksides shouting 'Thank you, thank you!' When he arrived back in England, however, he was simply asked whether or not he wanted to remain in the army and, when he said no, dismissed 'without one talk, one leaflet, one pamphlet, any guidance or advice about how to return to civilian life'. Dick Swarbrick, who had returned via San Francisco and New York to Southampton, had a happier experience: when he and twenty-six other local ex-POWs stepped off the train at Preston on 20 November, they found hundreds of relatives and friends waiting on the platform to greet them, accompanied by the mayor and a group of local officials. After handshakes all round and a brief welcoming address, the families surged through the barriers to welcome the men back, following which a shuttle service of eleven cars took them all to their homes.⁶

> Telephone: MAYFAIR 9400.
>
> Your Ref._____
>
> W.O. Ref. SS/330/120/224
> (Cas.P.W.)
> OS/3253/W
>
> THE WAR OFFICE,
> CURZON STREET HOUSE,
> CURZON STREET,
> LONDON, W.I.
>
> 28th September, 1945
>
> Madam,
>
> I am directed to inform you with pleasure that official information has been received that your **son, Lieutenant P.F. Given-Wilson, The Loyal Regiment** previously a prisoner of war in Japanese hands, has been recovered and is now with the Allied Forces.
>
> The repatriation of recovered prisoners of war is being given highest priority, but it will be appreciated that some time must elapse before they reach the United Kingdom. Information of a general character regarding these recovered prisoners, including their movements before they reach home, will be given from time to time on the wireless and will be published in the press.
>
> I am,
> Madam,
> Your obedient Servant,
>
> [signature]
>
> Mrs. S. Given-Wilson,
> 105, Cadogan Gardens,
> LONDON, S.W.3.

Letter to my grandmother informing her of my father's recovery from captivity

PRISONER STORIES

'My first uncensored letter for three and a half years!'

On 26 August, while still at Keijo, my father wrote a letter to his mother:

> Dear Mummy,
>
> This is my first uncensored letter for three and a half years! As you can see I'm beginning it while still in jug. To relieve any anxieties you may have, I am very fit indeed, and just longing to get out. We hope it will be soon. After a few days of terrific excitement we are trying to settle down while patiently waiting for someone to take us away. Any kind of work I find absolutely impossible, but fortunately we now have a good lot of novels.
>
> According to their lights [*his emphasis*] the Japs treated us well. I have no real animosity against them, apart from their system as a whole and an odd individual. As I mentioned in my letters about a year and a half ago, they stopped our newspapers, a bitter blow because nothing helped us more to keep cheerful than a knowledge of how the war was going. We knew of course that it was going well, but we wanted more definite news. We heard of Germany's surrender the day after they packed up. I tried to convey this in my letter to you, do you remember: 'Poor Uncle Fritz, I hope he is well'?
>
> This transition period is very unsettling. We have had our excitement and now all we want is to get away. Although there is of course no garden party now, we still get newspapers and are quite up to date. We also get plenty of rumours; 'Russian army arriving tomorrow', 'Americans landing in planes today', and so on. It's amazing how rumours spring up in a place like this. As yet we have no idea when we will go, how or by what route. I hope to go via America. It will be a good opportunity to see the States, where we will be welcomed. We are of course

feeding comparatively well now, getting our tummies into trim for a reasonable diet. This proves a slow and difficult business.

That's all now. I hope this letter will be continued in pleasanter surroundings.

[However, he was still at Keijo on 7 September, when he took up where he had left off]:

Three American officers arrived in our camp this morning having flown from Okinawa yesterday. They are dealing with POWs and collecting letters soon for dispatch by air. These Americans are the advance party of the army of occupation and it was a grand sight to see them driven into the camp. They tell us they hope to evacuate us by ship in two or three days' time. We are going to Manila.

The planes came at last on 29th and 30th and dropped supplies by parachutes. They had a difficult time as the camp area is very small, our exercise yard being the size of a tennis court and surrounded by slums. None of the stuff fell in the camp, some packets got loose from their chutes and quite a lot of damage was caused to houses nearby. Unfortunately, one old Korean woman was killed.

The Japs now started organising sightseeing trips by lorry. I went on one on the afternoon of the 3rd into the country by the river. It was great fun to be almost free and out in the open. We went boating and swimming. My first swim for over three years.

On the 5th fifteen officers (mostly those who could speak French, including myself) were invited to the French Consulate where we had a wonderful party – civilized food and drinks, no Japs around, etc. Mme Venjoz the consul's wife was very attractive, intelligent and an admirable hostess. It was a real joy to see her young children, white, clean and well clothed, a sight for sore eyes.

On the 6th was our Roman Catholic party at the cathedral. I needn't tell you how happy I was to go to confession, serve mass and take Holy Communion again after nearly two years. We took Monsignor Quinlan along afterwards to the cemetery where he held a short service for the R. C. dead, including Jackie Whiting, a friend of mine from the Singapore days who occupied the next floor space to me till he died a few months after arrival here from diphtheria.

The letters are just being collected so I'll finish now. Don't worry about my health, I am very fit indeed, I hope you are too. Goodbye for the present.

All love, Patrick

Arriving home at the end of October, my father embraced his new-found freedom like a puppy unleashed. Engaged within five months, married within twelve, he brought my mother back to Singapore, where he continued to work in the insurance business for the next eleven years. Perhaps surprisingly, they chose to live at Pasir Panjang, where he must have been reminded almost daily of those desperate last days in February 1942 when he and his fellow Loyals had fought to repel the Japanese onslaught on the city. Yet I never recall him speaking of that time, and hardly ever of his years at Keijo, even once I was old enough to have remembered. Like other FEPOWs, he simply wanted to forget. It was not my father but my mother who told me about *Nor Iron Bars*.

It is of course impossible to calculate with any precision the mental scars inflicted by three and a half years of humiliation and incarceration, but by the time I came to know my father, the breezy, clubbable 'Paddy' suggested by a succession of jaunty letters to his widowed mother in the years before the war – for he had been in the Far East since January 1937 – had been superseded by the kindly but rather cautious and diffident 'Patrick', and some of the stuffing seemed to have been knocked out of him. Of course, this could simply have been the passing of youthful exuberance, but he may also have suffered from survivor's guilt, as many FEPOWs did. Although he was taciturn on the subject of his imprisonment, my mother told me that he often had nightmares about it. He died in 1972, at the relatively young age of fifty-seven. Not many prisoners of the Japanese survived into old age.

RETROSPECT

'The hinge of fate'

JAPAN'S TREATMENT OF ITS PRISONERS OF WAR is usually explained by a combination of factors, one of which was the contempt which they felt for men who had surrendered rather than fight to the death. Japanese soldiers, in contrast, 'seemed almost to *want* to die for their country', a source of both trepidation and admiration to their opponents. Their emblem was the cherry blossom, which bloomed spectacularly but briefly before falling at the height of its glory. Habituated to the spartan rigours of Imperial Army discipline, they also despised Allied POWs for their constant demands for more food, greater comforts and respite from hard physical labour. In their view, the British and Americans had been degenerated by the decadence of their lifestyle: they wanted to wage a 'luxury war', reliant on the superiority of their materiel rather than the heroism of their soldiery, but without their ice-cream and their extravagant weaponry they simply crumbled. Put simply, they lacked moral fibre. The Japanese, by contrast, were resilient, sustained by their devotion to the emperor, their traditional values of duty, conformity and self-sacrifice, and their death-defying bravery. The 442nd Infantry Regiment, the most decorated unit in United States military history, was composed almost entirely of second-generation Americans of Japanese descent.[1]

Japanese soldiers also believed passionately in the cause that the emperor personified, the liberation of East Asia from Western colonialism. Fuelled by decades of anti-Western propaganda, they knew only too well how it was that Europe and America had acquired the wealth and mastery to bestride the globe. From the early seventeenth century to the late nineteenth, while Japan turned in upon itself, recoiling in self-imposed isolation from engagement with the world beyond its shores, European nations had busied themselves assembling the most far-flung empires the world has seen. From the early nineteenth century, the United States too joined the party – indeed it was the American Commodore Matthew Perry, arriving in Tokyo Bay with four 'black ships' in July 1853 to demand that Japan open its ports to Western traders, who set in motion the process that would shake the island nation out of its slumber.[2] And when Japan eventually emerged, blinking, into the late nineteenth century, what it discovered was a neighbourhood under the political and economic mastery of nations whose homelands lay five or six thousand miles away: the French in Indochina, the Spanish (followed by the Americans) in the Philippines, the British in Malaya, the Dutch in the East Indies, and all of them, to a greater or lesser degree, sprinkled across China, nested like cuckoos in their international settlements and long-lease concessions. It was as if the British had awoken from a long sleep to find themselves gazing across the Channel at a European mainland reduced to the plaything of rival powers from, say, India, China or Africa, subjugating its peoples and exploiting its resources.

The fact that Japan itself was not colonised doubtless had much to do with the 'closed country' (*sakoku*) policy it had followed since the 1630s. Once it ceased to be its own world state, however, it embarked on a high-speed dash towards parity with the West (though not without vigorous opposition from those who saw the influence of Western individualism and decadence as subverting the country's traditional values). 'Rich nation, strong army', argued the modernisers: only by assimilating Western technological and military know-how would Japan find the long-term security it craved.[3] And for the moment, the West appeared to welcome Japan's headlong plunge into the modern world, its attention diverted by the prospect of economic gain and fascination with a new and exotic civilization. For the moment, Japan was not seen as a military threat to Western interests in Asia, at least not by Britain, with whom it concluded an alliance in 1902. This was the first time that an Asiatic country had become formally allied to one of the great Western powers, a source of no little pride to the Japanese.

Closer to home, however, Japan's neighbours were becoming ever more concerned at its burgeoning economic and military capability, manifested by now in an alarmingly interventionist role in East Asian affairs. The Sino-Japanese war of 1894–5 led to Japan's occupation of Formosa (Taiwan), the Pescadores islands, and a number of bases in Manchuria and north China; the Russo–Japanese war of 1904–5 to the occupation of the southern half of Sakhalin island and (in 1910) the annexation of Korea; and the First World War, in which Japan sided with the Allies, to the seizure of Germany's colonies in the Shantung peninsula (China) and the Micronesian islands in the South Pacific. Thus, while Japan's public rhetoric remained resolutely anti-imperialist, the practical effect of its policies during the first two decades of the twentieth century was the creation of the first non-Western empire of modern times.[4] Yet this upstart empire was different from the opportunistic global agglomerations of the European powers. Shaped by strategic decisions at the highest level, its genesis lay not in the initial incursions of conquistadors, missionaries or traders, subsequently cemented into place by state-sponsored military might ('a state in the disguise of a merchant' was Edmund Burke's verdict on the East India Company), but in Japanese government policy. This was a regional empire, assembled to service Japan's perceived economic and security requirements. This also meant that, in contrast to Western empires in Asia, there existed a cultural affinity between the motherland and its colonies and a common desire to be free of European domination and to retain the resources of East Asia for the benefit of its peoples. This, at any rate, was how successive Japanese governments justified their acquisitions and eventually led them to propose the 'Greater East Asia Co-Prosperity Sphere' (*Dai Toa Kyoeiken*), a clarion call to which it was hoped that the region would respond.

Japan's transformation within fifty years from a quasi-feudal global irrelevance to what the 1910 edition of the *Encyclopaedia Britannica* described as 'an empire of East Asia, one of the great civilised powers of the world' was astonishing.[5] Already, however, there was talk of the 'Yellow Peril', and within another decade

Western concern at just how far this was likely to go had fanned out. At the Washington conference of 1921–2, Japan was forced to restrict the size of its capital ship tonnage, and in 1923 Britain abrogated the Anglo–Japanese alliance.[6] Seen by many in Japan as an act of betrayal by a trusted friend, Britain's rebuff 'inflicted a wound received in sorrow and remembered in wrath'.[7] Ten years later, following the Japanese occupation of Manchuria, the League of Nations denounced Japan as an aggressor and refused to recognise its new puppet state (renamed Manchukuo). Infuriated, the Japanese withdrew from the League, followed in October by Nazi Germany.

The decade that followed saw Japanese politics lurch sharply to the right. Stung by its perceived slighting as an outcast nation, the country retreated into ultra-nationalism. Party politicians gave way to admirals and generals, political violence intensified, and three prime ministers were assassinated. Renewed emphasis on the imperial cult went hand in hand with strident assertions of Japanese racial superiority.[8] By 1937, spending on a universal conscription army and a rapidly-expanding navy was accounting for almost fifty per cent of the country's national budget.[9] Yet its vulnerability was all too apparent: mobilization on such a scale demanded vast quantities of natural resources, especially oil, and by the late 1930s Japan was importing eighty per cent of its oil from the United States. Little wonder, then, that it began to cast greedy eyes in the direction of the vast oilfields controlled by the Dutch in the East Indies – Java, Sumatra and Borneo. But here too lay a problem: any attack on the East Indies would be doomed unless Singapore and the Philippines could be neutralised, for if Japan were to attack the Dutch, the United States and Britain would surely not stand aside. There were many in Tokyo, including Emperor Hirohito, who urged caution.

By the time full-scale hostilities with China erupted in August 1937, however, Japan was a nation in thrall to its Rising Sun, and after war broke out in Europe in September 1939, quickly laying bare the vulnerability of Hitler's European rivals, the opportunity to pursue its destiny in Asia became irresistible. The major remaining obstacle was, of course, the United States, but if a crippling initial blow could be struck at American naval power in the Pacific, there was a chance that Japan could buy enough time to realise what it saw as its legitimate aspirations. That it could not hope to win a protracted struggle was well understood, but how long might it have to wait until another such favourable combination of circumstances presented itself? As 1940 drew to a close, therefore, with Hitler still carrying all before him in Europe, Japan tilted decisively towards war. In September, the Tripartite Pact with Germany and Italy was concluded. In June 1941 Germany invaded the Soviet Union, forcing Stalin to transfer troops from the Pacific arena to the war in Europe. With its security concerns in the north allayed, Japan promptly occupied southern Indochina, a move which the French government, now under German control, did nothing to resist. To President Roosevelt, however, such a flagrant statement of intent could not be ignored, and in July he imposed an embargo on the export of oil to Japan. Nothing short of a declaration of war could have been better calculated to make the Japanese government realize that it was now or never. According to a report presented to the war cabinet in Tokyo, the nation's oil reserves would allow it to pursue its military ambitions for two years, after which, unless new sources were found, it would be left 'like a fish in a pond from which the water was gradually being drained away'.[10]

The plan for a pre-emptive strike on the American Pacific fleet was the reluctant brainchild of Admiral Yamamoto, commander-in-chief of the Combined Japanese Fleet and a specialist in naval aviation.[11] A graduate of Harvard and an outspoken critic of both the China war and the Tripartite Pact, he had deep misgivings about pushing the United States into war, but believed that if it were to be done, the initial blow must be overwhelming. And when the former army minister, Hideki Tojo, a punctilious strategist and strident advocate of war, became prime minister on 18 October 1941, the plan was quickly endorsed. The final decision for war was made at an imperial conference on 1 December, with the date set for one week later. Tojo knew as well as anybody that it was a gamble: 'The empire,' he declared as the conference broke up, 'is on the threshold of glory or oblivion.'[12] At 6.00 a.m. on 8 December,[13] the first of 353 bombers and fighters began taking off from carriers 250 miles north of Hawaii. The last radio communication before the outbreak of the Pacific War was received from the commander of the lead squadron at 7.49: 'Tora! Tora! Tora!' – indicating that they had avoided detection. Six minutes later, the first bombs fell on Pearl Harbor.[14]

If this helps to explain why the Japanese went to war in December 1941, it does not begin to justify their cruelty towards POWs, which remains for many a stain on the soul of the nation. They had signed (although not ratified) the 1929 Geneva Convention on the obligations of captors towards their prisoners, had agreed at the outset of the war to observe it, and were subsequently warned on numerous occasions that those who were found guilty of violating it would pay a heavy price once the war was over.[15] Yet even in 1944–5, as defeat and retribution turned from a probability to a certainty, they continued to commit grotesque barbarities against both POWs and the populations of the territories they had conquered in 1941–2. At the Tokyo and Yokohama war crimes trials of 1946–48, 920 Japanese were sentenced to death by hanging and around 3,000 to imprisonment with hard labour.

The relative moderation of the camp administration at Keijo meant that many of the Loyals did not, or at least professed not to, share the 'searing hatred' of the Japanese felt by most Allied POWs. 'I don't hate the Japs and I don't think the other fellows do,' wrote John Lever in March 1945. However, he may have been protesting too much, for he then went on: 'You wouldn't say that you hated a lot of irritating insects or a mean-natured cur. Detest and despise are better words. They are too small to be favoured with the word hate.' *Nor Iron Bars* is peppered with sneers at the Japanese as 'little monkeys', 'toads', 'squirts', or 'the short and yellow Nip', with his 'slant eyes centrally lopsided, of Asian types the worst'. *Zen* and *bushido*, articles of faith to many Japanese, were objects of amusement if not derision. 'Time for all loyal Japanese to polish up their *bushido*', commented Lever snidely as the Pacific War turned decisively in the Allies' favour. Once a week, when the guards commandeered the exercise-yard for marching or singing or bayonet practice, the POWs would surreptitiously watch the 'bayonet apes' and snigger: their marching was 'a shambles', their singing 'a sort of gurgle with a range of about one octave', and they thought that thrusting a bayonet into a sack of straw turned them, as one mock-sonneteer put it, into 'Hero-Gods':

> Behold the present masters of our fate,
> Dull, pompous, ignorant and never merry.
> The Gods Almighty of the second rate,
> Puffed up with self-conceit and beriberi.
> Eager to copy all the West has taught,
> Giving the world no music, art or science.
> Their one attempt at something new in thought
> Expressed in some weird Kobe sex appliance.[16]
> Born and brought up on protein-lacking rice,
> Half-formed in feature, this squat, shambling nation
> Lives but to breed and multiply like lice,
> With bestial grunts that pass for conversation.
> Doubters of Darwin's theory gape and blink,
> Dazed when confronted with the Missing Link.

No opportunity was lost to mock the vaunted virtues of Zen and bushido (*NIB*)

Although understandable in the circumstances, such sentiments were characteristic of the monochrome vision of the colonial ruler, evidence of that effortless disdain which the Japanese had come to associate with the Western masters of East Asia. Neither side in the Pacific War had a monopoly on racism. Most of the British in the Far East were as fully convinced of their own racial superiority as the Japanese were of theirs. Henling Wade, who was largely brought up in China, speculated that had the British been more willing to put their trust in the Malays and Chinese who made up the vast majority of Malaya's population, Japan's invasion of the peninsula in 1941–2 might have had a different outcome. Soon after their arrival at Keijo, one of the Japanese guards told Wade that Japan was prepared to fight for a hundred years to attain 'the liberation of all Asiatics from the white barbarians'. When it came to it, however, 'liberation' from Western dominance proved to be not a 'Greater East Asia Co-Prosperity Sphere' but the inauguration of an 'empire of the lash'.[17] Civilian deaths attributable to brutality or neglect in countries occupied by Japan between 1937 and 1945 are impossible to calculate exactly but are generally estimated at between ten and twenty million, three-quarters of them in China. The number of Western POWs who died building the Death Railway has been carefully calculated: 6,318 British, 2,646 Australians, 2,490 Dutch and 132 Americans, a total of nearly 12,000. The number of Thai and Burmese 'coolies' who died building it has been variously estimated at between 75,000 and 100,000, but no one was really counting.[18]

Four years on from Pearl Harbor, Japan lay in ruins, its scorched and shattered homeland occupied, its conquests amputated: not the glory on which Tojo had gambled, but the oblivion he had feared. Having failed to commit suicide, he was tried for multiple war crimes and hanged on 23 December 1948. Yet if Japan had unquestionably lost the war, it did not entirely lose the peace. In 1952, seven years after the war ended, the influential Japanese politician Masanobu Tsuji, who had served as General Yamashita's Director of Operations and Planning during the invasion of Malaya, published his memoir of the war, concluding as follows:

> We were severely defeated. But, as if by magic, India, Pakistan, Ceylon, Burma, the Dutch East Indies, and the Philippine Islands one after another gained independence overnight. The reduction of Singapore was indeed the hinge of fate for the peoples of Asia.[19]

Had he been writing ten years later, Tsuji's list of newly-independent nations in Asia (as well as Africa) could have been greatly expanded – including, among others, Malaysia and Singapore. For the victorious Allies, World War II tends to be remembered as a war of states, but to the Japanese it resembled more closely a war of empires. In the war of states, Japan failed utterly: rather than becoming the leader of a great Co-Prosperity Sphere, it surrendered the dominance in East Asia – and more specifically the dominance over China – which it had been striving for half a century to achieve. In the broader, longer view, however, Japan had dealt a fatal blow to the European empires in Asia, whose aura of moral and racial superiority had been irreparably shattered by their humiliating failure to protect the peoples whom they claimed to rule. It was not the new world that Japan had hoped to create, but it was nevertheless a new world.[20]

Bibliography

Barrett, John, *We Were There: Australian Soldiers of World War II* (Viking: Ringwood, Victoria, 1987)
Daws, Gavan, *Prisoners of the Japanese* (Scribe Publications: Victoria, 2004)
Encyclopaedia Britannica, 11th edition (Cambridge University Press: Cambridge, 1911)
Farrell, Brian, *The Defence and Fall of Singapore* (Tempus: Stroud, 2005)
Frei, Henry, *Guns of February: Ordinary Japanese Soldiers' Views of the Malayan Campaign and the Fall of Singapore* (Singapore University Press: Singapore, 2004)
Hane, Mikiso, *Japan: A Short History* (Oneworld: Michigan, 2000)
Havers, R. P., *Reassessing the Japanese Prisoner of War Experience* (Routledge: London, 2003)
Kennedy, Malcolm, *A History of Japan* (Weidenfeld & Nicolson: London, 1963)
Kirby, Stanley Woodburn, *The War Against Japan* (HMSO: London, 1957)
Kovner, Sarah, 'Allied POWs in Korea: Life and Death during the Pacific War', in *DJE*, pp. 107–24
Kushner, B., and S. Muminov (eds) *The Dismantling of Japan's Empire in East Asia* (*DJE*), (Routledge: Oxford, 2017)
Lomax, Eric, *The Railway Man* (Jonathan Cape: London, 1995)
Long, Gavin, *The Final Campaigns* (Australian War Memorial: Canberra, 1963)
Lu, David J. (ed.), *Japan: A documentary History: The Late Tokugawa Period to the Present* (Routledge: New York, 1997)
Odgers, George, *The Air War Against Japan 1943–45* (Australian War Memorial: Canberra, 1957)
Parkes, Meg, and Geoff Gill, *Captive Memories: Starvation, Disease, Survival* (Carnegie Publishing: Lancaster, 2015)
Piccigallo, Philip, *The Japanese on Trial: Allied War Crimes Operations in the East 1945–51* (University of Texas Press: Austin, 1979)
Storry, R., *A History of Modern Japan* (Penguin: London, 1960)
Tsuji, Masanobu, *Japan's Greatest Victory, Britain's Greatest Defeat* (The History Press: Cheltenham, 2001)

Wade, Tom Henling, *Prisoner of the Japanese: from Changi to Tokyo* (Kangaroo Press: Kenthurst, Australia, 1994)
Wigmore, Lionel, *The Japanese Thrust* (Australian War Memorial, Canberra, 1968)
Wilson, Sandra, 'The Shifting Politics of Guilt: The Campaign for the Release of Japanese War Criminals', in *DJE,* pp. 87–106

Web sites

Dick Swarbrick's War, https://www.far-eastern-heroes.org.uk/Richard_Swarbricks_War/index.htm
Eldredge, S., *Captive Audiences, Captive Performers* (Digital Commons @ Macalester College, 2014)
'The Loyal Regiment' https://www.cofepow.org.uk/armed-forces-stories-list/the-loyal-regiment

Endnotes

Preface

1. Stephen Bull, *Nor Iron Bars: Lancashire Artists in Captivity 1942–1945* (Lancaster, 2005). It is surprising that Henling Wade of the Loyals, one of the three editors of *NIB* until his transfer to a camp in Japan in November 1943, barely mentions it in his 1994 memoir, *Prisoner of the Japanese: from Changi to Tokyo*.

Chapter 1

1. 'The Loyal Regiment': https://www.cofepow.org.uk/ armed-forces-stories-list/ the-loyal-regiment.
2. *STS*, pp. 418–19; *POJ*, p. 167.
3. See below, Chapter Four.
4. Naturally this figure excludes the Nazi-run concentration camps.
5. *Captive Memories*, pp. 163–5.
6. *DFS*, p. 435.
7. Webber was later a POW on the Thailand–Burma railway, where he and his brother built and maintained a secret radio, for which he was subsequently awarded the OBE.
8. *CED*, pp. 61–2.
9. Hawaii is on the other side of the International Date Line, eighteen hours behind Singapore, so the attack on Pearl Harbour was timed at 8.00 a.m. on 7 December.
10. *WAJ*, p. 192.
11. The destroyers did however manage to pick up some 2,120 survivors, whose rescue was not impeded by the Japanese.
12. *DFS*, pp. 473–7; *WAJ*, pp. 521–7. For example, only about 26,640 were initially landed in Thailand and Malaya on 8 December.
13. Report on 'The Loyals in Singapore and Malaya' in LIM, p. 6.
14. *WAJ*, p. 243.
15. *DFS*, pp. 232–9; *WAJ*, pp. 274–81.
16. *DFS*, p. 359.

17 *DFS*, pp. 206–8.
18 23 officers and 489 'other ranks' ('The Loyal Regiment').
19 Col. Elrington, 'The 2nd Battalion in the Malayan Campaign: Sacrificial Encounter', in the Regimental Journal, *The Lancashire Lad*, March 1948, pp. 133–41; see also 'The Loyal Regiment'.
20 *DFS*, 287–96; *WAJ*, 315–16. This case later helped to convict General Nishimura, commander of the Imperial Guards; he was executed by hanging in 1951 for war crimes.
21 'Dick Swarbrick's War', chapter 3, 'Japanese Invade'.
22 Building of the base was begun in the 1920s but only finished in 1938.
23 *DFS*, pp. 328, 359.
24 *DFS*, p. 433.
25 These messages were actually sent to General Wavell, over-all commander in the Far East, and passed on by him to Percival: *DFS*, pp. 333, 405.
26 *DFS*, p. 428; *WAJ*, pp. 169–70.
27 CED, pp. 61–2.
28 *DFS*, p. 429.
29 *WAJ*, pp. 414–15; *DFS*, pp. 434–6.
30 Henry Frei, *Guns of February: Ordinary Japanese Soldiers' Views of the Malayan Campaign and the Fall of Singapore* (Singapore, 2004), pp. viii–ix, 30–1, 76–9, 86, 130–1, 155–7, 160–1.

Chapter 2

1 *NIB*, April–May 1942; *STS*, pp. 29, 34.
2 *STS*, pp. 38–9.
3 *NIB*, April–June 1942.
4 *STS*, pp. 325–43; Parkes and Gill, *Captive Memories*, p. 30.
5 *POJ*, chapter 11.
6 *SPK*; 'The Loyal Regiment'.
7 *IDS*; Lionel Wigmore, *The Japanese Thrust* (Australian War Memorial: Canberra, 1968), pp. 612–13.
8 JLD, September 1942.
9 *NIB*, Christmas 1942.
10 JLD, October 1942; *SPK*.
11 *NIB*, Christmas 1942.
12 Latrine (Malay).
13 For Starkey's story, see https://www.cofepow.org.uk/armed-forces-stories-list/the-fakai-maru.

Chapter 3

1 *NIB*, February 1943, Christmas 1944.
2 *NIB*, Christmas 1943, Christmas 1944, April 1945; *POJ*, chapter 12.
3 *NIB*, April 1943, July 1943, Christmas 1943, April 1945; JLD, December 1942, July 1943; *POJ*, pp. 58–60.

4 *NIB*, April 1943, Christmas 1943.
5 *NIB*, January, February and April 1943.
6 JLD, October 1942.
7 *NIB*, July 1943, Christmas 1943, Easter 1944, Christmas 1944.
8 *NIB*, Christmas 1944, April 1945; JLD, November 1944.
9 The POWs' way of describing Japanese-style drill; this poem is in *NIB*, January 1943.
10 *NIB*, July 1942, Christmas 1943, Easter 1944, Christmas 1944; JLD, April 1944.
11 *NIB*, April 1942, February 1943, July 1943; JLD, February 1943.
12 *NIB*, April 1943; JLD, July 1943.
13 Sarah Kovner, 'Allied POWs in Korea: Life and Death during the Pacific War', in *DJE*.
14 *NIB*, April 1943, Christmas 1943; JLD, November 1942, November 1943, May 1944, November 1944, June 1945, July 1945.
15 *NIB*, Christmas 1942.
16 *NIB*, Easter 1944.
17 *POJ*, p. 65.
18 *POJ*, chapter 15; JLD, December 1942.
19 JLD, January 1944.
20 *NIB*, Christmas 1943, Christmas 1945; JLD, November 1944; IMT, p. 51.
21 *NIB*, Christmas 1944; JLD, June 1944, October 1944.
22 There are lists of Loyals' deaths and burials in Korea in LIM.
23 *POJ*, p. 57.
24 *NIB*, February 1943.
25 *POJ*, p. 59.
26 Malay for 'left-overs'.
27 *NIB*, February 1943.
28 Punt's memoir, *Kura!*, written under the pseudonym Cornel Lumière, was published in 1966 (Jacaranda Press, Australia). This story is told in *STS*, p. 207.
29 *POJ*, p. 95.
30 *NIB*, December 1944.
31 *NIB*, April 1943.
32 *POJ*, p. 96.
33 John Barrett, *We Were There: Australian Soldiers of World War II* (Viking: Ringwood, Victoria, 1987), pp. 265, 351, 367; Gavan Daws, *Prisoners of the Japanese* (Scribe Publications: Victoria, 2004), p. 314.
34 Daws, *Prisoners of the Japanese*, p. 125; Parkes and Gill, *Captive Memories*, p. 70.
35 R. P. Havers, *Reassessing the Japanese Prisoner of War Experience* (Routledge: London, 2003); S. Eldredge, *Captive Audiences, Captive Performers* (Digital Commons @ Macalester College, 2014).
36 *POJ*, p. 40.

Chapter 4

1. *POJ*, pp. 75–6.
2. IMT, pp. 44–5. The trial record says 'two hours later' but his death was registered on 15 October 1942.
3. Keijo Camp Liberation Report (LIM).
4. IMT, p. 75.
5. See the conclusions of Philip Piccigallo, *The Japanese on Trial: Allied War Crimes Operations in the East 1945–51* (Austin, Texas, 1979).
6. JLD, July 1944.
7. IMT, p. 33.
8. IMT, pp. 17, 31.
9. IMT, p. 33.
10. JLD, July 1943.
11. IMT, p. 47.
12. IMT, p. 58.
13. IMT, p. 33. For further cases of officers being struck see *NIB*, Easter 1944, Christmas 1944; JLD, July 1944.
14. JLD, April 1944, October 1944; *NIB*, Easter 1944; *POJ*, p. 100; IMT, pp. 50–52, 80.
15. *STS*, pp. 130, 158, 357–9, 374, 441; *POJ*, chapter 21 and p. 178.
16. IMT, p. 49.
17. IMT, p. 34.
18. IMT, pp. 48–9.
19. IMT, pp. 34, 76.
20. IMT, pp. 49–50.
21. Prime Minister Tojo.
22. JLD, January 1944, October 1944; IMT, pp. 49–50.
23. Piccigallo, *The Japanese on Trial*, p. 85.
24. Kovner, 'Allied POWs in Korea'.
25. *STS*, p. 70.
26. JLD, April 1944, April 1945.
27. JLD, October 1944.
28. IMT, pp. 47–51.
29. *POJ*, p. 77; Kovner, 'Allied POWs in Korea'.
30. Kovner, 'Allied POWs in Korea'.
31. Sandra Wilson, 'The Shifting Politics of Guilt: The Campaign for the Release of Japanese War Criminals', in *DJE*, pp. 87–106.
32. IMT, pp. 4, 35–40, 53, 8–9, 76, 81; Kovner, 'Allied POWs in Korea', pp. 116–18.
33. IMT, p. 36.

Chapter 5

1. Kovner, 'Allied POWs in Korea'.
2. *STS*, pp. 352, 395, claims there were only four such show camps.

Woosung and Lunghua, its nearby civilian internment camp, are the setting for J. G. Ballard's novel *Empire of the Sun* (also a Steven Spielberg film). A few other camps on the Japanese mainland also received at least one ICRC visit.

3   Kovner, 'Allied POWs in Korea'.
4   *POJ*, p. 77.
5   Kovner, 'Allied POWs in Korea'.
6   *NIB*, Christmas 1942.
7   Elrington was in hospital from 24 February to 10 May 1943; he was hospitalised again on 18 Nov 1944 (*NIB*, April 1943, July 1943, Christmas 1944).
8   *POJ*, pp. 58, 85.
9   'Dick Swarbrick's War', chapter 3.
10 CED, p. 61.
11 As recalled by Henling Wade in *POJ*, p. 59.
12 *POJ*, pp. 76, 87, 175.
13 *STS*, pp. 33–4, 297–322.
14 'Dick Swarbrick's War', chapter 4.
15 Along with Colonels Crook and Dyson, who were not Loyals.
16 JLD, March 1944, July 1944.
17 *STS*, pp. 73–4.
18 JLD, November 1942, January 1943, January 1944.
19 *POJ*, p. 73.
20 *POJ*, pp. 11–12.
21 *STS*, pp. 67–91 (Toosey), 138–49, 297 (Dillon). After the war, Toosey was also active in helping to organise FEPOW clubs until his death in 1975 (Parkes and Gill, *Captive Memories*, pp. 5–6, 52, 233–4).
22 JLD, April 1944.
23 JLD, February 1943.
24 *NIB*, Christmas 1944; JLD, October 1944, July 1945.
25 *NIB*, Christmas 1944, April 1945; JLD, May 1945. After a reading of *Henry V* in March 1945, Shakespeare's plays were banned.
26 *NIB*, February 1943, July 1943; JLD, December 1942, May 1944.
27 *NIB*, April 1943, July 1943; JLD, June 1943.
28 *NIB*, April 1943, April 1945; JLD, November 1942, January 1945.
29 Kovner, 'Allied POWs in Korea'.
30 *NIB*, July 1943; JLD, December 1943.
31 *NIB*, Christmas 1943, Christmas 1944.
32 JLD, October 1944.
33 *NIB*, April 1943, July 1943, Easter 1944, Christmas 1944, April 1945; JLD, March 1943, May 1943, July 1943, May 1944, July 1944; *POJ*, p. 70.
34 *NIB*, Christmas 1944, April 1945; JLD, January 1944, October 1944, January 1945, April 1945, June 1945, August 1945.

Chapter 6

1. *NIB*, February 1943.
2. *STS*, pp. 287–96; Eric Lomax, *The Railway Man* (London, 1995).
3. *NIB*, January 1943.
4. JLD, November 1942, February 1943.
5. *NIB*, April 1943.
6. JLD, September 1943.
7. JLD, November 1943; *POJ*, chapter 14.
8. JLD, March 1943, June 1943, January 1944.
9. *NIB*, July 1943.
10. *NIB*, April 1943.
11. *NIB*, July 1943.
12. *NIB*, Christmas 1943.
13. JLD, July 1943, August 1943.
14. *NIB*, April 1944.
15. JLD, April 1944, June 1944.
16. This was very risky for all involved, and when the Korean boy visited the camp after liberation, he was warmly thanked and given a haversack full of Red Cross goodies. George Baker knew at least six languages. Lt Stewart Bell's 1944 Christmas card to him read: 'The toast "Release" I'll give in Greek/The only tongue you cannot speak' (Information from Richard Baker and documents in LIM); JLD, August 1945.
17. *NIB*, Christmas 1944.
18. *NIB*, April 1945.
19. JLD, March 1945.
20. JLD, July 1945.
21. JLD, June 1945.
22. JLD, March 1944; *NIB*, Christmas 1943.
23. JLD, May 1945.
24. JLD, January 1945.
25. *NIB*, Christmas 1943.
26. *STS*, p. 33.
27. *NIB*, April 1943.
28. *NIB*, April 1945.
29. *NIB*, Easter 1944.
30. *NIB*, April 1945.
31. *NIB*, Christmas 1944.
32. *POJ*, p. 166; *STS*, p. 432; Kovner, 'Allied POWs in Korea'; Parkes and Gill, *Captive Memories*, p. 147.
33. Letter from my father to his mother, 26 August 1945 (see below, pp. 126–8).
34. *STS*, p. 420.
35. *POJ*, p. 40.
36. *NIB*, April 1942.

Chapter 7

1. Letter from my father to his mother, 26 August 1945; JLD, August 1945.
2. *WAJ*, pp. 205–20.
3. Letter from my father to his mother, 7 September 1945.
4. *STS*, pp. 2, 16–22, 114–58, 344–54, 359, 377, 388; Parkes and Gill, *Captive Memories*, p. 87.
5. Letter sent from Manila, 19 September 1945.
6. *POJ*, p. 180; 'Dick Swarbrick's War', chapter 9, 'Going Home'. For the initial failure to provide ongoing medical care for returning FEPOWs, see Parkes and Gill, *Captive Memories*, p. 168.

Retrospect

1. https://en.wikipedia.org/wiki/442nd_Infantry_Regiment_(United_States).
2. M. Kennedy, *A History of Japan* (London, 1963), pp. 134–9; Mikiso Hane, *Japan: A Short History* (Michigan, 2000), pp. 34–46.
3. Hane, *Short History of Japan*, p. 84 (quote).
4. *CHJ*, pp. 217–21.
5. *Encyclopaedia Britannica*, 11th edition (1910), vol. xv, p. 156.
6. Capital ship tonnage was to be restricted according to the formula 5:5:3 (Britain: United States: Japan).
7. R. Storry, *A History of Modern Japan* (Penguin: London, 1960), p. 164.
8. Hane, *Short History of Japan*, p. 123; *CHJ*, p. 97.
9. Kennedy, *History of Japan*, p. 270.
10. David J. Lu (ed.), *Japan: A documentary History: The Late Tokugawa Period to the Present* (New York, 1997), pp. 425–35 (dated 5 November 1941); *CHJ*, pp. 333–4, 485; Hane, *Short History of Japan*, p. 163 (quote).
11. *CHJ*, pp. 330–2.
12. *CHJ*, p. 339.
13. 7 December in Hawaii.
14. 'Tora! Tora! Tora!', literally 'Tiger! Tiger! Tiger!', was in this case the agreed signal for 'surprise attack' or 'lightning attack' (*to*sugeki *ra*igeki).
15. Piccigallo, *The Japanese on Trial*, pp. 3–5.
16. The Arita Drug and Rubber Goods Company in Kobe, Japan, was well known for its manufacture of sexual aids, a box of which dating from the 1930s was recently exhibited at the Science Museum, London (https://wellcomecollection.org/works/j7u8wpr2).
17. *CHJ*, p. 269; *POJ*, p. 62.
18. *STS* gives differing figures, of 'perhaps 100,000' (p. 2), or 'at least 73,000' (p. 163); Parkes and Gill, *Captive Memories*, p. 26.
19. M. Tsuji, *Japan's Greatest Victory, Britain's Greatest Defeat* (Cheltenham, 2001), p. 281.
20. Cf. *WAJ*, p. 435; *CHJ*, p. 10.